SHOW ME YOUR MAD FACE

Teaching Children to Feel Angry without Losing Control

Connie J. Schnoes, Ph.D.

BOYS TOWN
Press

Boys Town, Nebraska

Show Me Your Mad Face
Published by Boys Town Press
14100 Crawford St.
Boys Town, NE 68010

Copyright © 2012, Father Flanagan's Boys' Home
ISBN 978-1-934490-31-0

Boys Town Press is the publishing division of Boys Town, a national organization serving children and families.

Publisher's Cataloging-in-Publication Data

Schnoes, Connie J.

Show me your mad face : teaching children to feel angry without losing control / Connie J. Schnoes. -- Boys Town, NE : Boys Town Press, c2012.

    p. ; cm.

    ISBN: 978-1-934490-31-0

    1. Anger in children. 2. Temper tantrums in children. 3. Child rearing. 4. Parenting. 5. Conflict (Psychology) in children. I. Title.

BF723.A4 S36 2012
649/.64--dc23   1202

10 9 8 7 6 5 4 3 2 1

Boys Town National Hotline[SM]
1-800-448-3000
A crisis, resource and referral number for kids and parents.

Dedication

This book is dedicated to:

My parents James Pruss and Marilyn Pruss Julian for encouraging me from early on to be assertive.

Whitney, Jordan, Morgan, Paige, Abby and Colin. God gifted me with each of you and you have each helped me to become the parent I am today. You are each amazing individuals.

My exceptional husband Dan. I can't imagine a more loving and devoted father and husband. Thank you for the family we are.

Acknowledgments

To all of the children, teens, and parents who have trusted me to assist them as they live their lives. You have helped me learn and grow and become a better psychologist and human being.

Thank you to Boys Town, for the opportunity and support that made *Show Me Your Mad Face* possible. To Pat Friman, you have taught me far more than you will ever know and I thank you for that. To my colleagues for teaching me something every day and allowing me to use all that I learn from you. I have the best job in the most remarkable organization. To Mike Sterba for helping me put my thoughts and ideas into words and making sense of my writing.

Table of Contents

INTRODUCTION 1

SECTION I: ANGRY CHILDREN

CHAPTER 1: Children and Emotions 13

CHAPTER 2: Children and Anger 21

CHAPTER 3: How Children Learn 29

CHAPTER 4: Why Are Children Angry? 41

SECTION II: WHAT PARENTS CAN DO

CHAPTER 5: Become a Better Parent 53

CHAPTER 6: Catch Kids Being Good 75

CHAPTER 7: Set a Good Example 85

CHAPTER 8: Consequences Work, So Use Them 89

CHAPTER 9: Listen to and Talk with Your Children 99

CHAPTER 10: Where Is Your Line in the Sand? 115

CHAPTER 11: Teach Ahead of Time 121

CHAPTER 12: "I'm So Angry I Could...!" Now What? 133

CHAPTER 13: Media Matter! 147

CHAPTER 14: Teach Problem Solving 157

CHAPTER 15: Know Where Your Children Are 163

CHAPTER 16: The Role of Spirituality 167

SECTION III: TEACH SO YOUR CHILDREN WILL LEARN

CHAPTER 17: Take a Teaching Approach 177

CHAPTER 18: When Children Lose Control 191

CHAPTER 19: When It's More than Just Anger 213

Index 217

INTRODUCTION

As I approached Cathy and her parents in the lobby of the Clinic, Cathy's parents appeared conflicted with several different emotions. They looked weary but relieved, hesitant yet hopeful, apologetic but appreciative. They returned my greeting and handshake with an uncertain urgency. I greeted twelve-year-old Cathy and extended my hand, but she ignored me: no eye contact, handshake, or an acknowledgment of any kind that I was even present. As I accompanied the family to a Clinic room, Cathy briefly looked my way with a facial expression that clearly told me she had no interest in attending the appointment or meeting with any kind of therapist.

In the Clinic room, Cathy demanded a certain seat and her parents relented. As the session began, she made it clear she had no intention of participating. She avoided my questions by saying with great annoyance, "I don't know" or "That's none of your business." Cathy's parents hesitantly answered my questions. With each answer, Cathy interrupted, all the while scowling and glaring at them, denying her parents' descriptions and challenging their accuracy on every detail. Her parents looked at each other, shrugging their shoulders and shaking their heads, then looked at me with exasperated expressions that said, "This is exactly what we're talking about!"

To me, Cathy was obviously angry and had anger control problems. According to her parents, she had been like that for years. In the past, they had consulted with their pediatrician and met with a number of other counselors and therapists. Each time, Cathy resisted and refused help.

Toward the end of the session, Cathy's parents described to me just how difficult it was to get Cathy to the appointment. On the drive over, she kicked, yelled, and screamed the whole way. She also threw her shoes and other objects to the front of the car. When they arrived, Cathy refused to get out of the car; she did so only after her parents threatened to call the police.

As we scheduled the next appointment, Cathy stood up and shouted, "I won't come back here again and you can't make me!"

• • •

Is Cathy an "angry child?" Some people wouldn't hesitate to give her that label, but I'm not so sure they would be correct. What I am sure of is that Cathy is a child who is angry. Is Cathy angry like other children are shy or outgoing? Her parents likely think of Cathy that way; however, I am reluctant to do so. There is much more to Cathy than anger and the ways she expresses it, and it's important for me to remain open and objective as I get to know all of Cathy better. Thinking of her as an "angry child" would narrow my perception of her and influence how I work with her and her parents.

I am a psychologist at Boys Town and currently work at Boys Town's Center for Behavioral Health (or the "Clinic") in Omaha, Nebraska. Since 1986, I have worked with troubled children and their families in various settings, including treatment foster care, inpatient psychiatric hospitals, residential treatment, and currently outpatient therapy.

Many of the hundreds of children I've been privileged to work with were angry and had trouble managing their anger. How do children move from child-like innocence to routinely being angry? And how can these children "unlearn" the angry behaviors they have come to depend on? There are no easy answers to these questions, making the task of figuring out how to deal with anger even more difficult. However, the kids and families I've worked with on a regular basis have reported that their kids' anger issues do improve over time if they implement and use the strategies discussed in this book.

What you will read in this book is based on my training and work experiences as a psychologist. My time at Boys Town has been one of the most significant influences in my professional development. The positive, skill-focused approach to helping troubled children and families overcome their problems, including anger, that lies at the heart of the Boys Town Model has influenced how I go about working with children and their families.

Many youth, including kids with anger and aggression problems, who come to the Clinic or to other Boys Town programs and services have learned how to control their anger, frustration, disappointment, and other unpleasant feelings and respond in new, appropriate ways that enable them to lead happy, calmer lives. The approach and the strategies described in this book can work for you and your child, too.

A Professional and a Parent

As children have participated in the Clinic's services, I have watched them learn to respond to difficult situations with emotions other than anger and manage their anger effectively. And parents have expressed gratitude and appreciation for the change, growth, and progress they've witnessed in their children.

I'm also a parent. My husband, Dan, and I have been married for twenty-eight years and are the proud parents of six wonderful children. Today, they range in ages from sixteen to twenty-five years. They are alike in many ways but very different in other ways. Genetics, temperament, birth order, and life experiences all contribute to these similarities and differences. Generally, they are all happy, healthy children.

As a parent, I have witnessed firsthand as my own children at times have chosen anger over joy in a variety of situations. For example, when they were young, most of my children enjoyed being silly, joking around, and laughing while one particular child seemed to take offense. She refused to participate in the fun or even smile or giggle. Instead, she would storm out of the room. Or, when some of my kids would recall silly or embarrassing moments, they would laugh and joke with each other. This daughter, however, would become angry, glare at the others, and say things like, "Shut up!"

Looking back, and given my training and experience, I know Dan and I influenced and shaped our children's behaviors. Even though all our children are generally happy, I can't help but think that early on, Dan and I gave considerable attention to our daughter's angry behavior. Our efforts to console, cheer up, and educate her likely served as potent reinforcement for her angry behavior. This helped to shape it into a surefire way to gain the attention of well-meaning, loving parents who only wanted the best for their child. As her angry responses increased in frequency, so did our responses and attention. Eventually, we consoled her less and reprimanded her more – all the while delivering a lot of attention that unintentionally reinforced her angry behavior.

As my daughter approached her sixteenth birthday, I was hopeful for a "sweet 16" transformation. A few months prior to her birthday, I began giving her spontaneous, unsolicited attention when she was not angry in the forms of hugs, compliments, statements of gratitude, and verbal affection: "I love you." "Have a great day." At first, her responses were stiff and limited. Gradually, they became more warm and welcoming, and she even began to return the attention and affection. I was pleased to see that the "sweet 16" transformation actually did happen.

I picked these strategies to use with my daughter because I love her. Clearly, the ways I was communicating my love for her were insufficient. She, like all of us, longs to feel loved, appreciated, and accepted. However, it is difficult to show love and affection for others when we do not feel loved and accepted in return.

From time to time, our daughter's angry behavior still creeps back in and causes problems, but Dan and I continue to work with and love her so she can become the best person she can be. Ultimately, I do not believe Dan and I are responsible for our daughter's behaviors – angry or otherwise. Instead, I believe the opposite is true: She is responsible for her behavior. However, I do know that as parents, Dan and I have a tremendous amount of influence on the choices all our kids make, just as you do with your children.

How This Book Can Help You and Your Child

As a parent, grandparent, or guardian, you are responsible for helping your children choose the right path as they grow up and join the larger society. That path can sometimes be rocky, with challenges and obstacles that must be overcome. That's where Boys Town can help. The goals of this book are to:

- Help you recognize angry behavior in your children and act before it becomes a problem.

- Show how you can teach your children to stop using angry or aggressive behaviors and learn new, positive behaviors.

- Help you better understand the child who is often angry.

- Provide you with information that can help you learn what your child's anger might represent.

- Give you strategies for influencing your child's behavior.

- Give you information about when it's a good idea to seek professional help for a child who is often angry.

This book is not about showing you how to teach your children to never get angry again. Recently, I had a client, a ten-year-old girl, tell me that one of her goals for therapy was to not get angry anymore. I told her that anger is a natural emotion, that everyone gets angry, and that we can't prevent or eliminate feeling angry. Instead, a more realistic and attainable goal is to learn how to manage and express anger in ways that won't cause problems in life.

We can't avoid feeling angry at times. It's unrealistic to think that we can prevent ourselves or our children from experiencing emotions. But we can control and be responsible for how we express our emotions, including anger. Just as laughing out loud and yelling with delight are not appropriate in all situations that evoke joy, hitting, yelling, and stomping away are not appropriate in all situations that evoke anger. But there are situations and circumstances when such angry responses may be appropriate and effective. For example, if a stranger is trying to lure a child into his car, yelling, hitting, and stomping might be the child's best responses. Granted this is an extreme example but it makes an important point: The circumstances of a situation and setting play a large part in determining whether behavior is acceptable or not. It's not just the child, the emotion, or how the emotion is expressed that determines whether behavior is appropriate and acceptable; rather, it's all of these things considered together.

When it comes to treating or dealing with anger, every child is different, and what works with one boy or girl might not work with another. There are no magic "cures." But that doesn't mean there isn't hope or solutions. Combined with a parent's love, the strategies described in this book can reduce angry behaviors and teach children that success is achieved through treating others with respect, kindness, and compassion.

Grandparents

Today, more and more grandparents find themselves in the position of having to parent their grandchildren. This can be due to parental divorce, mental illness, or death. Whatever the reason, parenting grandchildren poses unique challenges for grandparents and children.

Some grandparents might have primary parenting responsibilities for a significant amount of the time, while others might be the primary caregiver during week days, most days of the week, or fulltime. If you are in any of these positions, my hat is off to you. I look forward to being a grandmother someday. I envision visiting my grandchildren, watching them from time to time, and spoiling them, while their parents do the heavy lifting regarding parenting. It's healthy for children to have the kind of relationship I envision, but the reality is not all children get to have it.

If you find yourself in the position of having to parent your grandchildren, the information contained in this book will be as helpful to you as it is for parents. However, you will likely have a few additional and unique challenges to overcome, including:

- **You may prefer to grandparent rather than parent.** If you are a child's primary caregiver, you are the one responsible for parenting him or her. That means your job is to do all the teaching and managing of behavior. You may long to play with and spoil your grandchildren and they may wish for you to be a grandparent and not a parent. Even though you must carry the important responsibility of parenting and teaching grandchildren well, the good news is you can always make time for fun.

- **If you have to take on the parenting role for a grandchild, the relationship you and your grandchild have grown accustomed to will change.** Change in any relationship can be difficult. This is especially true when grandparents take on the parenting role with a grand-child whom they have already established a traditional grandparent-grandchild relationship with. The transition to a more parental role will be frustrating and difficult at times, but it's a necessary change to help your grandchild grow and succeed.

- **Children who are parented by grandparents fulltime must also adjust to the loss of their parents.** Obviously, infants and very young children won't be aware of the parents' absence, but older children and teens will. And, they will think of and come up with all kinds of explanations and reasons why they are now living with their grandparents. Some kids may think it is their fault their parents are no longer in their lives. These children are more likely to experience emotional and behavioral issues. The challenge here is that they may not often share these explanations and reasons with you. So, it's impor-tant for you to help your grandchild come to a healthy understanding of why he or she is now living with and being parented by you.

- **Grandparents who help parents raise their children face other challenges.** For example, grandparents might provide daily child care, grandchildren and their parents might live with grandparents, or the grandparent's home might be where regular visitation occurs with a non-custodial parent. Among the primary challenges in these kinds of situations is ensuring consistency regarding rules, discipline, decisions, privileges, and consequences. Children benefit and learn best when teaching is consis-tent from both parents and grandparents. So, as long as the parent's approach is healthy and safe, grandparents are encouraged to support, teach, and parent as similarly to the child's parents as possible.

If you are a grandparent in a parenting role, keep reading; I'm confident you'll benefit from the information here. Also, if you struggle with the challenges just discussed, I encourage you to seek out additional assistance and services. The task before you is not an easy one, and outside professional support can provide you with what you need to tackle these challenges in more effective and successful ways.

If you are a grandparent who is in a more traditional grandparent role, I would also encourage you to keep reading. If you have picked up this book, chances are you have a grandchild who struggles with managing anger. If that is the case, you will find helpful information and strategies for interacting with your grandchild. You might even encourage and recommend that your grandchild's parents read the book as well. One of the main goals of this book is to help all the adults (parents and grandparents) who care for children teach them how to better manage their anger so all involved can enjoy life more.

Parenting children with anger problems is especially challenging, and there are many unique difficulties along the way. I know because I've been there myself. But I'm here to tell you that you have what it takes! Your love, patience, and energy can go a long way but you also need ideas, techniques, and strategies like those presented here to help teach children more effective ways to express themselves and deal with people and situations that trigger feelings of anger. So let's begin the exciting journey of helping children transform their lives for the better!

SECTION I

ANGRY CHILDREN

CHAPTER 1

CHILDREN and EMOTIONS

Happy ... Sad ... Mad

These are just a few words people might use when asked to think of some emotions. Often, emotions like happiness, excitement, and cheerfulness are thought of as "positive emotions," while emotions like anger, sadness, and fear are considered "negative emotions." This kind of labeling suggests that some emotions are good, right, and acceptable to experience and express, while others are wrong, bad, and unacceptable to feel or express.

Thinking about emotions as positive or negative, right or wrong, or good or bad sets children up for a series of problems. Children might think that it is right to feel positive or good emotions and wrong to feel negative or bad emotions. Parents can reinforce this message and not even know it. For example, many parents work hard to make sure their children don't feel or experience negative emotions. Parents use strategies like distracting children from something that may upset them, consoling kids who become upset when they don't get their way, or appeasing tantrums by giving children what they want. At times, parents will do almost anything to calm, quiet, or cheer up their child. The problem when parents do this is that children learn that feeling and showing unpleasant emotions is unacceptable and makes others feel uncomfortable. Children also learn that showing these kinds of emotions can get them what they want – a tantrum gets them candy in the checkout lane at the grocery store, crying about the food they've been served gets them a preferred food, or expressing sadness about having to go to bed leads to staying up later.

Another problem with responding to emotions as negative or bad is the decrease in opportunities for children to experience and learn how to better express unpleasant emotions like anger, sadness, worry, frustration, fear, anxiety, grief, guilt, jealousy, and others. When parents and other adults work to prevent or quickly eliminate these kinds of emotional experiences for children, they don't learn how to effectively and independently manage these emotions. As a result, children don't learn how to "self-calm" or "self-soothe." Instead, they rely on others to do this for them.

Another difficulty that may result from emotions being labeled bad or wrong is the negative impact it has on a child's self-perception. For example, a child might think, "If I feel angry and angry is bad, then I am bad." Conversely, a child might also think, "If I feel happy and happy is good, then I am good." Is this kind of thinking logical? Perhaps. Is it accurate? Not even close.

It is important for children to learn that all feelings are okay and that what is important is how they are expressed. I recently worked with a mother and her two young sons following their father's unexpected death. As the mother shared information about this, her eyes filled with tears and her voice quivered. Her older eight-year-old son quickly said, "Mommy, don't cry." The mother tried to stop the tears, thinking this would be best for the boy. I spoke with her and her son about crying being normal and healthy, and that it is okay to cry when we are sad and even sometimes when we are happy. The mother's crying made the boy feel uncomfortable and there is nothing wrong or bad about that either. We all have to learn how to be okay with our own sad feelings as well as the sad feelings of others.

One of the first things I teach children and teenagers (in different ways) is that they don't get to choose how they are going to feel. They don't get to decide that they will never feel angry, sad, or worried again. Kids often come to our Clinic with this kind of goal or expectation. Once that faulty expectation is cleared up, we discuss what they do get to decide: How they express their feelings and what they will do with their feelings. So, if a child is angry, she gets to choose if she will yell and hit or if she will walk away and cool down.

When discussing emotions with kids, I keep the words "positive" and "negative" – and other words that label emotions as good or bad or right or wrong – out of my descriptions and discussions of emotions. Instead, I emphasize that all emotions are part of the human experience and that they help us live life more fully. For example, we wouldn't know what it's like to be happy if we never felt sad. Or, we wouldn't know what it's like to feel confident or proud if we didn't experience fear or embarrassment.

Feelings are the experience of emotions. Do we like to feel happy? Sure we do. Would we rather feel confident and relaxed than apprehensive and tense? Of course we would. It's just that working to never feel certain emotions is unrealistic and goes against human nature. That's why it's important for kids to learn that they are going to experience and feel a wide range of emotions, sometimes on a daily basis and certainly over a lifetime.

Emotions at Different Ages

Emotions serve different purposes for children at different developmental stages. When we hear an **infant** cry, we might instantly decide he or she is sad or mad. But infants aren't expressing emotions; instead, they are expressing discomfort from being hungry, having a wet diaper, an upset stomach, or gas, feeling cold or hot, being tired, or being in pain. When infants get physically uncomfortable, they lack the words to express their discomfort and are incapable of doing anything but crying about it. They need parents and other adults to determine and address their needs.

Similarly, smiles from infants are not expressions of happiness. Instead, they are expressions of physical comfort. Smiles and crying produce very different responses from adults in the infant's world. Generally, crying results in holding, bouncing, changing, feeding, or burping, while smiling results in cooing, talking, holding, and smiling from adults.

During "toddlerhood," children learn words and statements like "I love you" and "I hate you." They begin to use such phrases in situations where they are experiencing emotions, and they get reactions from the adults around them. Toddlers don't yet understand what it means to "hate" or "love;" instead, they've heard the words and are trying them out in their own way. Parents are quick to assign the full meaning of these words and statements to their toddlers' intentions. In reality, toddlers don't have a clue what their words really mean. They are simply "trying them on" and seeing what happens. For example, saying "I love you" likely leads to hugs, smiles, and warm words in return from adults. Saying "I hate you" likely results in frowns, lectures, or adults telling the toddler their feelings are hurt. Both reactions are reinforcing and toddlers figure out what to continue to say and not say in the future. Ultimately, they are learning new ways to express their feelings of happiness, anger, and upset.

Once toddlers have expressed an emotion, they move on quickly. Due to their developmental stage, toddlers don't have the cognitive capacity to harbor feelings toward others. They simply go forward like nothing ever happened, because when the emotion and situation it was attached to is over, it's over. For example, when a parent drops a toddler or preschooler off at daycare or preschool and the child cries, the upset is typically over within minutes of the parent leaving. And the child doesn't keep thinking about the upset all day. Actually, the child later likely won't even remember crying that morning. Parents, however, often feel upset over their child's outburst for hours, if not days, weeks, or even years.

School-age children begin to develop a sense of the wide range of emotions they can experience. They are increasingly aware that others are forming impressions of them and their behavior. Like younger children, when an experience is over for school-age children, it is over and they move on. For example, when children feel mad, they are mad in the moment, and then they move on to whatever is next. Children have the ability to let go of emotions quickly, while adults tend to remember things and hold grudges.

It often seems as if teenagers tend to express their feelings of happiness, joy, and excitement with their friends, while saving and expressing feelings of anger, annoyance, and sadness with their parents. Adolescence also is a time when teens begin to discover creative ways to express their feelings through dress, hairstyles, make-up, music, writing, and drawing. In addition, teenagers identify with their emotions and with others who appear to experience emotions similarly.

Adolescence is a time when emotions begin to define the person rather than the person defining the emotions. It also is a time when the belief that emotions are "negative" or "positive" becomes a conscious way of thinking about emotions. Some might think "If I feel bad, I am bad," and this thinking can manifest itself in visible ways in their words and actions. For example, acts of self-harm like burning or superficial cutting are sometimes acts of self-punishment. A teen might be upset due to having made a mistake and self-harm is a way to punish and track his or her failures. Or, a teen might identify with a certain group, like "emo" or "goth," and begin to dress and act in accordance with others who identify with the group. Now, the teen isn't feeling sad or depressed, they are acting or behaving like they are sad or depressed.

Many teenagers think that something must be wrong with them if they feel sad, angry, anxious, jealous, or experience some other unpleasant feeling. As a psychologist, my goal is to help teenagers know that there isn't anything wrong with them or the various emotions they experience and feel. It's important to help them understand how this kind of thinking only makes them feel worse. And it also makes it more difficult for them to feel happy, confident, comfortable, grateful, and other more pleasant emotions.

What You Can Do

Your child models your behavior in all sorts of ways by watching what you do and say. And that includes how you manage your emotions. Many parents try to shield their child from unpleasant or difficult emotions (sadness, anger, frustration) they might be experiencing. Parents don't want their child to experience these unhappy emotions. However, this just results in lost opportunities for your child to learn from you. There's no better teaching opportunity for your child than watching you effectively handle difficult or unpleasant emotions by choosing to remain calm and/or optimistic. For example, when a loved one dies, it is okay (and even good) for children to see their parents cry in sadness over their loss. Or, when a parent gets cut off in traffic, it's powerful for a child to hear his or her parent say something like, "It really irritates me when people don't look before changing lanes," rather than yelling at and gesturing to the other driver. Or, when a teen comes home late, instead of quarrelling and dishing out negative consequences right then and there, a parent might instead say, "I am glad you are home safe. We will talk about the consequences for you being late in the morning. I love you. Good night."

Children often see poor examples of how to manage emotions. Some kids see parents or other adults yell, hit, drink alcohol, abuse drugs, or engage in other damaging behaviors when faced with challenging emotions. The danger here is that these children are likely to do and say the same things when faced with similar emotions. That's why it's important for you to always remember that your actions have an enormous impact and influence on your children and how they will react and behave.

Besides good modeling, there are other things you can do to help your child effectively manage his or her emotions, including:

- Accept that your child will experience all emotions and encourage him or her to experience them. Pay attention to your child and offer empathy for the emotions you see your child experiencing. For example, you might say things like: "You seem excited about your date." "You have been studying hard for your test and sound nervous about how you will do." "It's okay to be sad about your best friend moving away."

- Take an inventory of the emotions you are comfortable with your children experiencing and expressing and the emotions you work to have children avoid feeling, or don't want them to feel. For example, do you try to prevent your child from having tantrums? Or, what do you do when your teenager cries?

- Start small and increase your comfort level with the various emotions your child experiences. For example, if it's easier for you to let your child be upset about something at home instead of in public, deal with the issue or situation at home. Or, if you are able to let your teen work through frustration on his own but you feel compelled to step in when he is angry, then start by letting him deal with frustration on his own. The next time he shows signs of frustration pay attention, offer empathy, and praise his ability to handle it calmly when he does.

- Show empathy to your child by saying things like, "You seem frustrated" or "It's hard when you feel angry."

- Offer encouragement and suggestions for managing emotions. For example, you might say this to a child who is angry: "You are upset, but you're doing a great job of keeping your voice calm." Or, for the child who is frustrated, you might say, "I can see you are frustrated with your homework, but you are continuing to work hard to try and figure it out."

Ultimately, it is up to you to accept that it's okay for your children to feel and experience all emotions. Your job is to teach them effective ways to express and manage their emotions.

CHAPTER 2

CHiLDREn anD AnGER

Anger is a natural emotion that all humans experience. It is neither good nor bad; it's simply part of the human experience. According to the dictionary, anger is defined as "a strong feeling of displeasure…." Anger is a general term that conveys nothing about justification or manifestation; rather, it just describes the emotional reaction.

One way to think about anger is as a **primary emotion**. That means some people might consider anger as more acceptable to acknowledge. And, it is often expressed or experienced in place of **secondary emotions**, like frustration, embarrassment, worry, and even sadness. Let's look at an example of this: Imagine your teenage daughter, who historically has met her curfew, is late coming home on a Friday night. Earlier, she went out with friends, which included a group of girls and boys, to a movie. One of her friends drove. Currently, your daughter is ten minutes late, you've heard nothing from her, and she hasn't answered your calls or texts to her cell phone. Ten minutes later, you begin to experience surprise and irritation, along with a slight concern about her welfare. (Keep in mind this is the first time she has been late.) After another five minutes of unsuccessfully trying to reach her, you begin to become more concerned and start imagining different reasons why she is late. As the clock keeps ticking, you continue to have no luck contacting her and you become increasingly worried as your imagination takes you down the road of a car accident and an injury. At this point, you check in with other parents but still don't get any specific answers or information about your daughter's whereabouts. Suddenly, thirty minutes past her curfew, she strolls in the front door with a smile on her face, looks at you, and cheerfully says, "I'm home. The movie was great. I'm beat and going to bed."

In this scenario, there's a good chance you would experience anger and express it in your words and actions. You might blame your anger on your daughter being late and clueless that she is late. You also might think you are angry because she didn't call, answer her phone, or apologize to you. But these aren't really the sources of your emotional reaction. Instead, your underlying emotion – worry (a secondary emotion) – stems from your thoughts about her safety. Your anger flared in response to your daughter's lack of awareness about her actions, resulting in your anger crowding out your worry. Your worry about her safety was lost in your anger that she was late and gave no consideration to your feelings by failing to call or answer your attempts to contact her. It's almost as if you're angry because you had to worry. In this scenario, anger is the primary emotion and worry is the secondary emotion.

Here's another example from Clinic. I have been working with a thirteen-year-old boy who was very angry whenever he was with his parents. They described him as well-mannered, friendly, and a great kid at school and when he was around his grandparents. With his parents, however, he barely spoke to them, was rude (told them to "shut up"), and rarely responded to their questions. To me, he looked angry. And he said he was angry. What appeared to be beneath his anger (primary emotion), however, was fear (secondary emotion). This young boy exhibited numerous problems, including poor academic performance, lying about his activities with friends, aggression toward his brother and sister, and refusal to complete chores. His misbehavior resulted in criticism and consequences from his parents at pretty high rates. Eventually, the boy came to recognize that, while he was unhappy and angry about the negative consequences from his parents, he was really afraid that his parents didn't love him.

Young boys in particular seem to have a difficult time sharing that they are afraid, of not having any friends, of failing in school, or that their parent's criticism means they don't love them or they aren't good enough. For many of these kids, it's easier to avoid facing the fear and instead to express anger. With anger, the fault or blame is often placed on the parents, while fear really belongs to the child. And, it really isn't brave or "cool" in a boy's eyes to be afraid. Anger is "tough" and, therefore, more acceptable.

Anger is an emotion adults and children express more often, yet underneath it are other emotions, like frustration, embarrassment, worry, self-doubt, and others. Many people are unaware of and/or deny these kinds of secondary emotions. It's as though they believe that being angry is "safer" than being embarrassed or being vulnerable, and that anger is a "strong" emotion while the other emotions imply "weakness." In reality, it takes much more courage to express embarrassment, fear, or worry than it does anger.

The Blame Game

Another issue with anger is that it is often blamed on the other person (or persons) or the situation, while other secondary emotions are viewed as the responsibility of the person who is angry. It's common for people to think along these lines: "It's your fault I'm angry. If it wasn't for you, what you did, and what happened, I wouldn't be angry." This is a way to justify anger.

People do take responsibility for their secondary emotions, which are often masked by anger. For example, people think: "If I'm frustrated, anxious, or embarrassed, that's about me and my weaknesses."

Both of these lines of thought, however, are inaccurate. Ultimately, each of us is responsible for all the emotions, including anger, we feel and express. While we don't get to choose the emotions we experience at any given moment, each of us does get to decide how we will express our emotions. Others aren't responsible for making us feel certain ways, and they certainly aren't responsible for how we express our feelings and emotions. That means it is up to the individual to recognize how he or she feels about certain emotions and how to express those emotions.

Our thoughts and beliefs about emotions influence our expression of them. Messages like, "boys don't cry," "stop crying," or "I'll give you something to cry about" teach children certain emotions are okay to express or experience and others aren't. So, kids learn to ignore or avoid some emotions, thus failing to learn how to express them assertively. Helping children learn to recognize, label, and express all emotions is ideal. But, this isn't easy to do because in order to teach children to do this, parents must be able to do it themselves, too. And parents have their own learning histories when it come to recognizing, accepting, and expressing emotions.

With any emotion, difficulties do not arise from feeling or experiencing the emotion. Difficulties can arise from how the emotion is expressed. For example, even the expression of joy can result in problems if a teenager disrupts a quiet setting, like a library, with exuberant cheers, or a school-age child is unable to stop giggling when a teacher is delivering instructions. Of course, these examples are less problematic than the possible destructive or demeaning expressions that can come from a person who is angry, but they are essentially the same problem. The point here is that children and teens (and many adults) must learn to express all emotions effectively, respectfully, and assertively.

Emotions and Assertiveness

What is meant by expressing emotions assertively? I may be picking apart words but I think it is important here. It's not uncommon to hear the phrase "express emotions appropriately." The difficulty with the term **"appropriately"** is that its definition varies greatly from person to person and family to family, and it even carries different cultural implications. For example, in some families and cultures, fighting back is accepted and promoted when a child is wronged or bullied. The message is "don't let them push you around, fight back." In other families and cultures, the message is "turn the other cheek." So, depending on your values or perspective, individual families would defend their actions as appropriate.

Another phrase that is often used is "to express emotions **effectively.**" Here, you could argue that all emotional expressions are effective if an observer is able to determine what emotion is being expressed. However, that creates difficulties just like the term "appropriate." For example, yelling at and hitting someone may effectively express and communicate anger but it's not what we want to teach children to do to express anger.

That's why the approach of "expressing emotions **assertively**" works best. Assertiveness carries an accepted definition that recognizes and respects both the needs of the individual and those around him or her. Being assertive means protecting your own rights and getting your needs met without violating the rights of others. Being passive and being aggressive are on opposite ends of the spectrum, while assertiveness lies in the middle of the two.

Being passive means meeting the needs or rights of others to the disregard or violation of your own rights, while being aggressive means meeting your own needs or rights to the disregard of the needs or rights of others. Let's look at an example here: An angry child who is passive might blame herself for a problem or situation. She might say something like, "It's my fault my brother hit me. I shouldn't have told Mom and Dad he was up late." On the other end of the spectrum, an aggressive child who is angry might blame the other person (or persons) for the problem. So, the aggressive brother who is angry at being told on might say something like, "My sister shouldn't have told on me and deserved to be hit." In this scenario, a healthier, assertive response from the brother would be to tell his sister, "I am angry that you told on me," without any hitting or blaming. Of course, there might be emotion in the brother's voice tone, facial expressions, posture, and words, but there would not be any aggressive actions. Also, an assertive response the sister could use with her brother might be, "You staying up late kept me up late, too. I had every right to tell. And I know you're mad, but that's not my fault."

Helping Kids Express Emotions Assertively

One of the most important things you can do to help your child express emotions assertively is to model doing so yourself. The young boy I mentioned previously in the chapter provides a relevant example. When we talked about and explored the people modeling expressions of anger around him, it became clear he followed his parents' lead. They openly reported to me that they would become very visibly upset when angry. So, they committed to changing this behavior to help their son.

Another strategy involves allowing children to become angry so they can learn to manage this emotion and learn how to calm themselves down. (This strategy is discussed in more detail in Chapters 17 and 18.) And this recommendation isn't limited to just anger. The only way children can learn to manage any emotion is practice, and they can only really practice by experiencing the emotion.

A third approach involves providing children with clear, consistent expectations about what are acceptable assertive expressions of anger. This is done by delivering contingent consequences, positive and negative, based on the child's expression of anger. (This is discussed in more detail in later chapters.)

Finally, it is sometimes necessary is to seek professional help. Having another person who can help you and your child break current patterns of interactions, try new ways of interacting and communicating, and consider other perspectives can be extremely helpful. A professional also can help you increase your awareness of current family dynamics and develop new coping and problem-solving strategies to help your child or teen learn to manage anger assertively.

CHAPTER 3

HOW CHILDREN LEARN

Many parents bring their children – preschoolers, school-age kids, and teens – to the Clinic for help with problems related to anger. These parents express concern that their children can't control their anger, seem mad all the time, are defiant and aggressive, and break and hit things that sometimes result in injury to themselves. The descriptions of problems and what some children do when angry are as varied as the parents and children who come for help. However, the common denominator in all of this is anger.

By the time parents seek help, they are at a loss for what to do because they have tried everything they can think of. Parents' frustrations are high, patience is waning (and usually gone), and fear is setting in that something is really wrong with their child and that they are failing as parents.

What many parents need at this time is hope and reassurance. So, it's important for them to understand that everyone – children, teens, and adults – has to learn how to cope with and express feelings of anger in assertive and healthy ways. Humans are not born knowing how to do this. Instead, we learn how from our environment – from parents, family members, teachers, coaches, the media, the music we listen to, and from other people and resources important in our lives. All these environmental influences shape what we learn about handling and expressing feelings of anger.

Individual differences, like temperament, development and cognitive abilities, also impact what we learn and how fast we learn. But, the bottom line is that we have to learn – and we do that through experience. Learning happens whenever we engage in a behavior (whatever it is) and experience what happens afterwards. Notice I didn't say someone must first tell us how to do something and then we are able to do it. That really doesn't work when it comes to learning. Still, many people and institutions put a lot of stock into telling people how to do things. For example, much of our academic/educational systems (from preschool through university doctoral programs) are built on verbal instruction, reading how to do something, and watching others do it. While we do learn from these strategies, the most powerful strategies include "hands-on" learning.

The reality is we don't really learn a behavior and how to use it until we actually do the behavior for ourselves. For example, someone could explain to you how to play a piano, swing a golf club, or make a peanut butter and jelly sandwich. And you could even read about how to do all of these things and watch others do them. However, the real learning happens when you spend time doing each of them yourself.

Learning to express emotions involves the same process: Children and teens learn from their environment and role models and from actually experiencing emotions in various situations. That means, when a child's parents express anger by yelling and hitting, it's likely the child will use these same unhealthy and harmful behaviors. Since children are not born knowing how to express anger, it's important for you to give them opportunities to experience and, ultimately, learn how to express anger in ways that are appropriate and healthy for them and others.

Anger at Different Ages

Children of all ages experience and express anger; after all, it is a natural emotion that's part of the human experience. How children express anger varies from child to child and changes as kids age. The following are behaviors commonly seen from children at different ages in response to anger.

Toddlers

Very young children throw tantrums when they are angry. These tantrums can include one or more of the following behaviors: crossing their arms, bowing their head, pouting of the lip, being silent, whining, yelling, screaming, saying "No," banging their head, crying, saying hurtful statements, using foul language, falling to the floor, kicking, hitting, stomping, and throwing things. The difficulty with younger children is they express different emotions with similar acts. That means toddlers might tantrum when they are angry but also when they are sad, afraid, frustrated, hungry, tired, or disappointed.

Parents sometimes struggle to understand why their toddler throws tantrums. Many times, it seems to happen for no apparent reason. When examined more closely, something typically happens **before** the tantrum that leads to the tantrum behaviors. For example, a child might have been told "No," instructed to do something he didn't want to do, asked to stop a pleasant activity and do something less fun or interesting, or someone might have taken the child's toy or touched it. That's why it's important for you to pay attention to what happens before the tantrum takes place to help you determine why the child tantrums. Once you sort out what triggers tantrums, you can plan to create opportunities where the child can learn to better manage being angry.

Developmentally, toddlers have undergone incredible growth. They have learned to sit, stand, crawl, walk, and talk. They have figured out that people and objects continue to exist even when they are out of sight. Even with all of this growth, their brains will continue to develop until they are in their mid-twenties.

Language is one of the most misunderstood of toddler behaviors. Typically, developing toddlers have learned hundreds of words. What parents should remember is that while toddlers can say words, they don't understand the meaning of many of the words they use. Parents often think a toddler means everything she says and understands everything the parents say. Saying words is a simple motor skill, while understanding the meaning of words is related to brain development and cognitive abilities. Toddlers can say the word "die" but have zero understanding of the word's meaning and the finality of death. Similarly, when toddlers say "I hate you!" they are typically angry but do not comprehend the meaning of the statement in the same way older youth and adults do. Toddlers do, however, learn what happens next and how others respond to their words.

When addressing problem behavior and delivering negative consequences, parents are encouraged to say few words. A general guideline is to use one word for each year of the child's age. So for example, you might say, "No hitting, time-out," with a four-year old. Choose your words wisely and judiciously when disciplining toddlers. Often, parents want to talk with their child about her behavior and explain why it is wrong. You can do this, but save your words for a time when the child is not angry.

School-Age Children

As children age, they learn to express different emotions in different ways. The differences in their expressions may be subtle or more obvious. You might think about it much like your child's crying as an infant. Initially, all crying sounded the same. Eventually, you figured out that certain cries meant certain things, like pain, hunger, and emotional upset. School-age children are figuring out how to communicate their emotions more clearly. When sad, they begin to cry without yelling. And, they begin to show embarrassment (blushing, sheepish or star-tled expressions, etc.). Also, they may show fear by being quiet or by active refusal (declining invitations to do things, staying close to parents instead of venturing out, etc.) We think of these changes in emotional expression as coming with age, and they are to a degree. However, what's more important than age is developmental growth. That means, not all children develop in all areas at the same rate. Their brains continue to develop over time, especially the emotion center (or limbic system). This development accounts for their increased need to experi-ence and recognize a variety of emotions. Development of the emotion center occurs ahead of the development of the part of the brain that is responsible for logic and decision making (the prefrontal cortex).

School-age children continue to develop their vocabulary and with learning more words comes increased understanding of the meaning of words. These abilities continue to be mis-leading with adults as they treat and interact with school-age children as though they have the full developmental abilities of adults. In reality, they do not. School-age children's brains are not that developed yet, and their ability to think abstractly is particularly limited – and for younger school-age children even impossible. So be patient with your child and keep in mind that behavior is in part a reflection of the child's developmental level.

When angry, school-age children tend to yell, hit, name call, run off, stick their fingers in their ears, and say hurtful things. Those children who struggle to manage their anger might throw or break things and use foul language. These kinds of behaviors warrant immediate and firm attention and action from parents for kids to turn their behavior around. If your efforts seem to have little impact, you might consider outside help (parent training, psychological services). The quicker you address inappropriate behaviors (independently or with addi-tional help), the quicker they will change. Why? The more time a child spends using aggressive behaviors in ways that work, the more firmly established they become in the child's skill set. Also, it's important to address more mild negative behaviors readily and firmly. But, because they are not quite as extreme, parents often feel less concerned or eager to address these behaviors. Keep in mind, if you leave these less-severe expressions of anger unattended, the more likely they are to evolve into more problematic behaviors. Children don't just grow out of problem behaviors. They need their parents' assistance to teach, model, and manage their behavior.

Here's a list of some common events that might trigger anger in school-age children: not getting their way, being told "No," having rules enforced around homework, going to bed (or bedtime routine), having time spent with friends or on electronics restricted, being asked to complete chores, earning negative consequences for breaking rules or getting poor grades, and parents checking up on cell phone and Internet activities. Parents are encouraged to be diligent about doing all of these things even though it will likely upset their child. Remember, your child has to experience upset and anger in order to learn how to manage and express it assertively. If parents back off because children might become upset, they will figure out relatively quickly that anger works in getting their way. Reluctance to address your child's behavior may be another cue that it's time for you to seek outside help.

Teenagers

One significant and very common change that occurs as children enter adolescence is the change in who they prefer to spend their time with. Parents of teenagers know that teens prefer to be with and talk to their friends. I recall when my younger brother's oldest son turned thirteen. One day, my brother told me this about his son: "He turned thirteen and forgot how to talk to me and his mother. We get grunts." As parents, Dan and I actively said the following to each of our children as they entered adolescence (and we said this in a humorous but sincere way): "You are not allowed to stop talking to us when you are a teenager." Did that make a difference with our children? In some ways I believe it did. Why? Because we set an expectation. And we continued to talk with our children with the expectation and message that they would talk to us in return. Communication builds trust and with trust comes the increasing independence teens so desperately want. So, as our kids continued to talk with Dan and me, we increased their independence.

Teens become increasingly independent in many ways. They can stay home alone, hang out at the mall without parents present, go to movies without adults supervising them, etc. There is a huge shift in supervision, and parents often welcome this newfound freedom, too. But, teens actually need more supervision than when they were younger. Think about all the new things and activities teens have access to: smoking, drinking, drugs, sex, pornography, and many others. Parents don't have to let their teens be independent without supervision. You have the right to ensure their healthy development through supervision. Now, that doesn't mean, you should go with them to the movies. It does mean they have to ask your permission to go out with friends to some activity. And, you should get details such as who they will be with, what they will be doing, where they are going, when they will be back, how they are getting there, and what parents or adults will be around for younger teens. (In general, older teens tend to hang out in groups at the homes of other teens.)

As parents, Dan and I don't say "Yes" to our teen's request to go out unless and until we get all these details. Also, I encourage parents to check in on teens during their outings. In this age of cell phones and texting, you don't ever really know if your teen is being truthful about where he or she is unless you have a GPS on the phone. My oldest daughter figured this out long before cell phones were a mainstay. I recall one occasion where she had permission to drive her friends to a movie and then spend the night at one of the girl's homes. My daughter called from her friend's cell phone to say they were at her friend's home. However, the following Monday, we discovered she was not quite yet at her friend's home when she called. Instead, she was still out and had been up to some harmless teenage pranks that were nevertheless not okay (Store security cameras are great detection tools!). She earned consequences and lost our trust for a while.

Another change for teens is related to their brain development. The prefrontal cortex (or logic center) is still developing. So, at times, the teen seems quite logical and rational. An adolescent is able to see things from the point of view of others, relate to how others feel, and use logic to problem solve. However, when teens become upset, their emotion center (limbic system) takes over and their logic center (prefrontal cortex) pretty much shuts down. This inconsistent display of skills is difficult for parents, especially when a teen is upset. Parents want the teen to be rational and talk with them to discuss what happened, but the limbic system's dominance means emotion makes reasoning very difficult. Your best option is to set limits, talk less, and allow the teen time to calm down.

Now, let's talk about how teens express anger. Again, there is quite a wide range of expression that varies with each teen and his or her emotional development level. On the less extreme end, teens tend to yell, argue, become demanding ("I will hang out without whoever I want!"), and get defiant ("You can't tell me what to do!"). They might claim you are being unfair. They will likely let you know their friends' parents don't get mad about whatever it is that lead to the teen's anger outburst. And, teens will likely storm out of the room before you are finished "talking." More severe or problematic behaviors include swearing, threatening to be aggressive or leave the house, becoming aggressive (taking a swing at or hitting you), and throwing and breaking objects. Also, they may even take off out of the house. It is always important to address **all** these behaviors. If you don't, the milder behaviors will likely escalate into more severe behaviors. And, left unchecked, the more severe behaviors can lead to far more serious problems for you and your teen – injury, assault, police or social service involvement, etc. Again, if your efforts don't seem to be making much of a difference, seek professional help. I would recommend visiting with a behavioral psychologist or therapist. Also, you might consider joining a parenting class to help you learn more parenting skills.

Here's a list of some of the things that lead to teens becoming angry: questioning their newfound independence (in other words, being a parent!); following through with the expectation that they must report the who, what, where, when, and how information when they ask to go out; being asked about their social outings when they get home (or the next day); getting into trouble for coming home late; parents showing up and making sure teens are doing what they said they are planning to do (whether they see you there or not); monitoring grades, Internet, and cell phone; and other important parent supervision activities. It's really pretty simple: Anything parents do to supervise their teens tends to aggravate them and can lead to anger. Keep in mind that as you check up and check in with teens and discover them doing what they asked to do, the more you will develop trust in them.

Another important parent activity is to know your teen's friends, along with their parents (when you are able). It's not unreasonable to expect your teen to spend time with friends at your home. This is an excellent time to meet them and get to know them better. This also lets your teen's friends know you are paying attention and you care about your teen and his or her friends. Doing this can really help to deter problem behaviors.

Most of the behaviors discussed in the three age group are ones many people think are common expressions of anger (tantrums, yelling, swearing, hitting, throwing things, glaring, etc.). They are behaviors typically considered inappropriate and problematic. And they are usually the ones that parents notice because they are more obvious and "in your face."

The problem with only noticing these types of behaviors in response to anger is that other, more appropriate responses get lost and go unreinforced. For example, if a child takes a deep breath and calmly accepts criticism, hardly anyone notices that the child is angry. Parents may be relieved their child didn't throw a tantrum but they often don't say anything. As a result, this positive coping response is overlooked and the child doesn't receive any specific feedback or praise for staying calm. The absence of attention to staying calm serves to punish or decrease the likelihood the child will stay calm in the future.

Instead, what usually happens is the child receives criticism more often and more freely because he or she accepts it so well. The child's appropriate behavior makes it easier for others to give criticism, so they give it more. The risk here is that, over time, the increased criticism and attention to only what the child is doing wrong will likely result in the child being less able to appropriately manage anger. When this happens, the child's motivation to remain calm decreases, and the increased criticism leads to more angry responses. As the child reacts more negatively, others will avoid delivering criticism and the child will experience less criticism and anger.

The key point to remember here is that adults should pay attention to and provide praise whenever children use appropriate responses to anger. And, when they use inappropriate responses, adults should teach kids healthy, assertive responses. This positive teaching approach to behavior and how you can do it will be discussed in much more detail in later chapters.

Children Learn by What You Do

While it's tough for many adults to stay calm when angry, it's even more difficult for children. Yet some adults expect children who are angry to remain calm in their voice tone, words, and actions. These kids are expected to act like they aren't mad when they really are.

Imagine you are angry and others expect you to respond by calmly saying, "I am angry." Then, you're expected to stay in the anger-provoking situation and continue to respond appropriately. How easy is that for you to do? Now, imagine how hard that is for a child who doesn't have your skills and experiences.

Think of the last time you were angry – maybe someone cut you off in traffic or your child talked back to you. What did you do? Did you handle the situation well, let alone perfectly? While it is reasonable to pursue the goal of having children and teens respond calmly and assertively when angry, it's important to keep in mind that it will take time, patience, practice, and effort. After all, think how long you've been working at that yourself!

When it comes to your children learning how to assertively manage their anger, they have at least two things going for them:

- They have spent less time expressing anger the wrong way.
- They have parents who want to help them learn healthy, assertive ways to express their anger.

On the other hand, as parents, you have some things you are up against, including:

- When your anger shows up in problematic ways, your child learns from you. And children are far more likely to **do** what their parents do than what they **say**, especially when these two messages are different or in conflict.
- You have to manage yourself when your child is angry and chances are you will be angry, too.
- You have to allow, and sometimes create, opportunities for your children to be angry. And, you have to let them be angry and calm themselves down. It's important for children to learn how to self-calm and also how to self-soothe

so they can control their responses to anger. Many parents don't allow these things to happen and instead they try to calm their child by:

- holding, caressing, talking gently, and rocking.
- threatening, slapping, or spanking.
- distracting or appeasing by offering a toy, activity, or privilege.
- using humor to manage the problem.

The best place to start helping your children learn how to better manage their anger is to get a better handle on your own responses when angry. In Chapter 7, "Set a Good Example," we will discuss how you can go about doing that. This is an important step toward helping your child build a solid foundation for a healthy and successful life.

CHAPTER 4

WHY ARE CHILDREN ANGRY?

The youth I see in Clinic, whose parents have brought them in for problems with anger, have involved and complex histories of powerfully controlling others and situations through their use of anger. These children aren't angry people and don't necessarily want to be angry. Rather, they have **learned** through experience that expressing anger serves them well. It allows them to access or obtain an outcome they prefer and to manage people around them to do what they want them to.

Recall a time when you told someone "No" and the person didn't accept your answer. Instead, the person persisted with the request. For example, it might have been your young child wanting candy in the grocery store checkout line or a telemarketer trying to sell you something you didn't need or want. It can be exasperating when your "No" answer is not readily accepted, and it's difficult to follow through with your answer without getting angry. But, you don't have to get mad to communicate you mean "No"; instead, you simply have to stick to your decision.

With kids who have anger problems, being told "No" is a common trigger for angry and aggressive responses and behaviors. Other triggers include being instructed to do chores or some other task and getting in trouble for doing something wrong. An example many parents can relate to is when they tell their children or teens to shut off the cell phone and get ready for bed. Here, children are being told to do something they do not want to do, and they respond by becoming angry and yelling. They also might demand more time on the phone, complain about the rule of shutting off the cell phone at bedtime, argue for a later bedtime, defend more time on the phone by saying it's for homework help, or give any number of other reasons or excuses. What the child or teen says to you doesn't really matter. What is important in these situations is being committed to teaching your child how to following instructions and rules without becoming angry and reacting and behaving in inappropriate ways.

We Don't Know What We Don't Know

So why do people – kids and adults – get angry? Somewhere in our learning histories, we have experienced and learned that anger means we are serious – that we really mean what we are saying or doing, whatever that is. If we look at the examples just discussed, this kind of learning history becomes more evident. Chances are we have all had the experience of being on the phone with a telemarketer who continues to try to sell us something after we have politely and repeatedly said "No." It isn't until we sternly, emphatically, and angrily say "No" that the telemarketer finally relents and we can properly end the call without resorting to hanging up on the person.

This same learning history applies to your kids when you tell them "No." Their angry reaction and behavior often results in them getting what they want. For example, the child's anger at being asked to shut off the cell phone at bedtime might result in the parent giving the child another fifteen minutes on the phone, or the parent might become frustrated and walk away without enforcing the rule because she is at a loss for what else to do. Unfortunately, what happens here is the child learns that anger works. And since the child gets what he or she wanted, it is highly likely the child will use anger and aggression in the future with you and others.

This might sound a bit silly or obvious, but people don't know what they don't know. I think about the family I grew up in. I remember there were intense verbal conflicts between my parents, brothers, and sisters. And I remember lots of laughter and love, too. However, what I didn't know, because I didn't experience it, was that disagreements could be resolved without intense conflict or anger. I learned I didn't know this after meeting and spending time with my husband's parents. They were able to disagree without arguing or even getting angry or frustrated. I remember asking my husband, Dan, if his parents ever argued and he said, "Not really." That experience resulted in "new knowing" for me about how to better manage disagreements. You can provide this same kind of "new knowing" for your children in all sorts of situations, including those where they frequently get angry.

Children come to know about anger by engaging in actions and experiencing what happens as a result of those actions. Let's take a look at how this happens with three age groups.

Toddlers

Early experiences for toddlers typically involve not getting what they want when they want it. This might include "No" answers to requests for sweets or toys, or having their playtime interrupted due to bedtime. When these kinds of things happen, it's typical for toddlers to respond with a tantrum. When that happens and the toddler gets his way, it is highly likely he will throw tantrums in the future so he can get his way again. Over time, the toddler's parents might set fewer limits or give in more often and more quickly to the child's demands in order to avoid triggering tantrums. This pattern simply strengthens the power of tantrums and increases their frequency and intensity.

School-Age Children

As children reach school age, angry responses may include aggressive behaviors (words and actions), creating problems at school and home. At home, school-age children might throw things, slam doors, or tear their bedrooms apart when angry. Verbal aggression toward parents might include yelling ("Get out of my room!"), saying hurtful things ("I wish you weren't my parents!"), making threats ("I'll throw this at you!"), or some other angry reaction.

At school, children often exhibit less severe behavior. When they do show anger toward a teacher or an adult, they may say things like, "You can't make me!" Then they storm out of the classroom or refuse to answer or respond in any way when the teacher or adult addresses them.

Making mistakes on schoolwork or not being sure how to do an assignment might also trigger anger in some school-age children. Here, they might become sullen and refuse to work, tear up their paper and throw it away, or cry. Again, with these responses, anger serves to let children escape feeling embarrassed or to avoid doing work that is too difficult.

School-age children more commonly exhibit anger toward their peers. For example, a child may become angry while playing a game if he doesn't think others are playing fair, if he is losing, or if he makes a mistake. He might direct this anger toward another child by pushing, hitting, or name-calling. The angry child also might quit, storm off, or take the ball or other object needed to play the game and refuse to share or participate. In all these situations and responses, anger allows the child to escape feeling bad or feeling like he or she isn't any good at a game. Also, anger might lead to extra turns or getting other children to play the game the way the angry child wants it to be played.

At this point, it would be helpful to say a little something about bullying. Bullying is another way for children to get what they want (toys, money, notoriety, etc.) by force. Also, it's important to note that not all bullying is related to anger. Plenty of kids bully other kids for different reasons, including:

- It might make them feel "cool" or "tough."
- They might think it's funny to scare or intimidate other children.
- They might have learned that they can keep other kids from joining in on games or avoid sharing by being mean. Here, bullies may say things like, "You can't play with us." Or, they may simply not pick a classmate to be on a team.
- They might want what another child has so they take it away. For example, bullies may push their way in front of another student to be first in line or they might snatch a ball or toy from another child.

In these examples, it is unlikely that the bully is angry. Rather, he has simply found a way to get what he wants by being mean or using force.

The media often portray bullies as angry. And I am sure some children bully because they are angry. However, children learn ways to get what they want, and if being a bully or bullying other children out of anger or for another reason works for them, they will continue to use it.

The keys to changing or preventing bullying behaviors from becoming a pattern are to teach children better ways to get what they want, prevent bullying from working for them, and ensure that the negative consequences they earn for bullying outweigh the benefits. (For more detailed information on bullying and how to deal with it, see the Boys Town Press book, *No Room for Bullies.*)

Some school-age children might use aggression as a way to escape uncomfortable situations, like separating from a parent, doing challenging academic work, or performing in front of peers. Some children lack the skills and understanding necessary to successfully navigate social interactions, so they might take what they want from peers rather than asking and waiting. Other examples of aggressive acts typical of this age group include:

- When called a name, a child retaliates with verbal and/ or physical aggression, including name-calling, yelling, pushing, hitting, etc.

- When peers change the rules of a game or the child is losing a game, she gets quiet and accuses the others of cheating and unfair play.

Now, let's take a look at a couple of real-life examples from Clinic regarding how aggression can develop in school-age children. Recently, I began working with two elementary-age boys for behavior problems at school. One of the boys had a history of delayed language skills that likely contributed to his use of physical aggression to get or communicate what he wanted and needed. If he had schoolwork that was "too hard," he would tear up his paper. If his peers had a ball he wanted, he would take it away. If he wanted to be on the slide, he pushed his way into line. If someone wasn't walking fast enough in front of him, he shoved the other child. He seemed to be aware that other kids didn't particularly like him, but he wasn't aware that his aggressive behaviors were getting in the way of making and keeping friends.

The other boy frequently had "meltdowns" when told "No" or to do his homework. As I worked with him and his parents, they became increasingly aware of how they avoided creating situations that might trigger the boy's tantrums and aggressive behavior. They avoided telling him "No," often negotiated with him when he asked for things or activities, and pleaded with him to do his homework.

As you can see, both boys' aggressive behaviors got them what they wanted or helped them avoid doing something they didn't want to do.

Teens

For pre-adolescents and teens, anger is often exhibited as verbal and/or physical aggression. Youth in this age group may say things like, "I hate my life" or "I hope you die." Other angry statements that are more oppositional in nature include, "I'm not doing anything you say" and "I don't care what you say. I'm doing what I want!" Physical aggression might include shoving parents, pushing past them, raising a clenched fist toward them, throwing objects at parents, or throwing objects (cell phones, iPods, glass items, etc.) to break them.

Older kids typically use anger to access their privileges and avoid demands, like homework and chores. Adolescents who don't want to do chores or homework and who are doing poorly in school academically, usually find themselves in uncomfortable and tense situations with their parents. The parents want their kids to follow rules, help out at home, and get good grades. When teens don't do these things, tension and conflict occur.

For many teens and parents, there can be lots of conflict that involves anger on both sides. For example, I recently saw a seventeen-year-old boy and his mother. The teen reported having poor relationships with both of his parents, claiming that all they do is argue with him so he avoids talking to them. He viewed his parents as angry people and they viewed him as an angry teen. All this had been going on for many months. The parents were angry and given the circumstances, I wasn't surprised. After all, the teen was failing most of his classes, wasn't helping out at home at all, and was frequently out with friends, driving his car, and smoking and drinking.

The parents' anger wasn't getting them anywhere in terms of helping to change their son's behavior. However, voicing their anger did make them feel better because they felt like they were "doing" something. Their anger let their son know they didn't approve of his behavior. On the other hand, the son's anger served to let him escape from chores and homework, while also keeping all of his privileges. And because using aggressive words and actions got him exactly what he wanted, he was likely to use these behaviors again and again. In the end, the cost of the son's and parents' anger was a deteriorating relationship filled with tension, frustration, and conflict.

Getting to the Bottom of Your Child's Anger

As the parent of a child who is often angry, it probably feels like your child is **always** angry. I remember feeling and thinking that way about my daughter. But when I started paying closer attention, I discovered she wasn't always angry. Rather, she became angry in some situations or when certain things were going on around her. It helped to figure this out because then I could go about teaching her to manage herself differently when faced with those particular situations. This is an approach I frequently suggest parents use with their children.

A good place to start doing this is to pay attention to what happens just **before** the child becomes angry. Again, the most common triggers for children and teens include being told "No," being instructed to do a task, or being asked to stop a preferred activity. Kids like to get their way, just like anybody – adults included. With your kids, the hope is that by the time they reach adulthood, they have learned and developed skills for accepting and coping with situations in appropriate ways when they don't get what they want.

Once you have figured out your children's triggers for anger, you can begin to plan ways and opportunities to teach them how to respond differently. You also can manage certain situations more effectively so their anger doesn't work for them – meaning it doesn't get them what they want.

It's important for parents to be able to step back and watch their children's reactions without getting caught up in them. And, you should remind yourself that your task is to help your children learn to manage their anger better. You can look at their reactions to determine if they are making progress. If they are, it's important to praise them; if they aren't, continue teaching and practicing with them. This way of thinking helps parents remain calm and manage their children's behavior with a teaching approach that's positive and effective.

Sometimes, the triggers for a child's anger are more difficult to identify, or it might seem like the child is just generally angry or irritable. Here, parents need to respond to the child's anger in ways that let her know that the response is unacceptable. In addition, it might be necessary to seek outside help. It is not uncommon for children who experience anxiety or a depressed mood to display anger rather than worry or sadness. If you are unsure, mental health professionals can assist in determining whether or not this might be the case, and they can offer suggestions or recommendations for how to best proceed.

For many of you, it can be difficult and challenging to figure out what your child's anger is about and why he is angry. As we've discussed in this chapter, most times it's a learned behavior that helps children and teens get what they want and need. However, anger can also be more than a learned response, and the problems it can create at home and school can sometimes get too big for you to handle. If you have tried to help your child and nothing seems to be making a difference, keep reading and give some of the suggestions in the chapters that follow a try. If these don't improve or resolve the situation, I would encourage you to get another perspective and guidance from a child-care professional.

SECTION II

WHat PaRents can DO

CHAPTER 5

BECOME a BETTER PARENT

Parenting is not an easy job. In fact, it is probably one of the most difficult and demanding jobs a person can undertake. The phrase, "Kids don't come with instruction booklets," applies to all parents. There's so much at stake, yet there's very little preparation and direction regarding how to be a good, effective parent.

For some, parenting gets off to a relatively painless start. Their baby is mild-tempered, easy-going, and a good sleeper and eater. For others, however, the challenges can start immediately. For example, babies with high-strung temperaments become upset more easily and are more difficult to console. Some babies struggle to feed (or nurse) well or have allergies that may go undetected for a time and interfere with feeding. Then there are those babies who wake frequently throughout the night for feeding and/or changing, making getting sufficient rest challenging for the baby and parents alike.

Unlike other jobs you take on, there is no "time off" for parents, and you can't leave your parenting job at the office. Parenting goes with you everywhere and stays with you forever.

Each day, parents have a lot on their plates and their schedules are full. For most parents, the daily challenges increase as their children age, even when they develop without any particular medical, behavioral, emotional, or mental health problems. So, it is no surprise that parents with kids who have problems related to anger can feel frustrated and overwhelmed. After all, their daily challenges are multiplied and intensified.

For parents learning to cope with, teach to, discipline, and relate to children who are often angry, your job is particularly difficult. Doing this requires patience, consistency, perseverance, and understanding – all qualities and traits no one is capable of exhibiting at all times. Instead, it's normal and typical for you to feel and display other emotions like frustration, impatience, doubt, and guilt. That's why you need education, support, encouragement, and, at times, professional assistance in dealing with children.

Remember you are not alone and your situation is not unique or hopeless. There are things you can do. This chapter provides you with some approaches, ideas, and strategies you can use to help your child with his or her anger problems and make life less challenging and stressful for you, your child, and your family.

What Kind of Parent Do You Want To Be?

Parents grapple with many questions throughout their parenting experience, including: Are we being the kind of parents we want to be? Are we being good parents? Are we doing the right things as parents for our kids? There are many times and situations where parents are unsure if they said or did the correct and best thing for their children. While many uncertainties exist, parents do have control over deciding what kind of parenting style they want to have and use with their kids.

Much of what you say and do as a parent, you learned from your parents. Usually you parent your children as your parents raised you. For example, the discipline strategies you use may be similar to those your parents employed. So, if your parents spanked you as a child, you may think of spanking as acceptable. Or, if your parents encouraged your participation in activities outside of school like sports, music, dance, or drama, you may find you encourage your children to participate in similar activities. Or, if your parents made it a point to spend time with you playing, talking, or taking vacations, you may very well do the same with your kids.

When I look at how Dan and I parent our kids, it is interesting to note the differences. Often, I can see the relationship between our differences and the differences in how we were parented. For example, I have ten siblings in my family, and I am confident this impacted how my parents raised us. My siblings and I were encouraged to participate in sports and music. Music was more encouraged with the girls. However, we were limited to one sport each school year. This family "rule" (or expectation) changed as I reached high school and I was able to participate in several sport seasons and music, too. At the time, even though my siblings and I participated in sports, our parents rarely attended our events. I really didn't think much of them not being there, but I was always delighted when they were able to attend. Dan had a much different experience with his family and parents. He was encouraged to participate in sports all throughout the year. Also, his parents attended all of his games, with few exceptions.

As parents, Dan and I have agreed that our children benefit from participation in sports. I also favor additional participation in music, drama, and speech. While I have attended many of my kids' sporting events, I have never attended any of their practices (nor has Dan) and I do not feel guilty when I am unable to attend an event. Also, early on, when our older children were faced with scheduling conflicts between sports and other activities, there was typically a lean toward the sporting activity. I attributed this to my husband's experiences growing up. Now, however, our younger children are allowed to let sports come second to other activities when there are conflicts. This is much more in line and similar to my experience growing up. So, over time, there has been a change in our parenting perspective. Many parents have different parenting histories and experiences. When you have these differences, you and your spouse should come to an agreement on how to consistently handle situations in ways that are healthy for your children and family.

We discussed in an earlier chapter that "we don't know what we don't know." When it comes to parenting, parents often think that how they parent is how it "should" be done. And they aren't open to or don't realize there are other ways to parent that may be better for them, their children, and their families.

Let's take a look at some different parenting styles. See if you recognize yours. And see if there is a style you can choose to use that will help you parent more effectively and allow you to become a better parent, beyond what you have experienced and already know.

Parenting Styles

There are three general parenting styles: authoritarian, permissive, and authoritative. The first two, authoritarian and permissive, are considered less than ideal and present inherent problems and outcomes. Authoritative is considered the most effective and healthiest parenting style for parents to use with their children.

Authoritarian

Authoritarian parents are those who make all the decisions and choose not to take the child's point of view into consideration. This style tends to impede the development of the child's problem-solving and decision-making skills and abilities, and can damage the relationship between children and parents.

Let's take a look at two examples of this parenting style involving a child's clothing and a teen's friends. An authoritarian parent picks out the child's clothes and decides what she will wear each day. Typically, the child has little say in the type or style of clothing she prefers or in putting together outfits for any occasion (school, outings, or church). This can lead to conflicts between the parent and child over clothing and can impair the child's skills in learning how to independently choose appropriate dress for various occasions.

When it comes to friends, an authoritarian parent will restrict their child's friendships to only those peers the parent approves of. The criteria for approval varies with different parents and families. For example, it might be related to the potential friend's family reputation, the type of work his parents do, his activities and/or grades in school, the neighborhood or community he lives in, the church the friend attends, or any number of other criteria. The result, however, is the same: The teen is not allowed to identify potential friends, get to know them, and make informed decisions about whether or not to maintain a relationship. Typically, this leads to problems, including:

- Conflicts between the teen and parents.
- Potential sneaking around by the teen to see the peers the parents don't approved of.
- Impaired skill development related to deciding what qualities make a good friend.
- Decreased social opportunities.

Permissive

Permissive parenting is on the opposite end of the parenting-style spectrum. Here, parents make decisions based solely on the child's wants; there is little to no consideration given to the parent's point of view. This style can produce children who are self-centered, unable to delay gratification, and have poor frustration tolerance.

Let's take a look at this parenting style using the same two issues previously presented. For the child and clothing choice, the permissive parent lets the child freely decide what she wants from stores and what to wear each day. This can result in the child demanding certain brand names and styles of clothing, or picking clothes that may be inappropriate for the weather or occasion. Efforts by the parent to provide limits or guidance are met with tantrums and disruptive behavior, and the parent readily relents to the child's demands. Over time, the child may choose clothing the parent finds increasingly inappropriate but the parent might feel like he or she has no control over or influence on the child's clothing choices.

Now, let's look at the teen and friends issue. Permissive parents provide little if any oversight regarding who their child is spending time with and what the child and his friends are doing. Permissive parents may be unaware of who their teen is hanging out with. This may result in the child spending time with peers who may engage in inappropriate or illegal activities. Any efforts by the parents to set limits in response to their teen getting into trouble are met with opposition and defiance. The teen simply walks out of the house and continues to do what he chooses. The parents may be aware of the problems but feel helpless with regard to influencing their teen's behavior and choice of friends.

Authoritative

The authoritative parenting style works well because it balances the child's perspective with the parent's perspective, so both viewpoints are considered when making decisions and solving problems. This style promotes healthy development of the child's abilities and skills regarding decision making, teamwork, and problem solving, and it also enhances the parent-child relationship.

Using the same examples, authoritative parents involve their child in decision making that's appropriate to their developmental level. So, they might identify clothing options before purchasing them and allow the child to make the final selection. As the child ages, the parents may allow the child to identify clothing but the parents must first approve the clothing before it is purchased. By the time the child becomes a teen, she understands and knows what her parents would likely approve or disapprove of and is able to shop independently and make acceptable and appropriate purchases. When it comes to picking out clothing outfits, a similar progression takes place with kids and their parents.

When it comes to the teen and friends, authoritative parents provide oversight, supervision, and guidance. They assert themselves and set the expectation that they must meet the peers their teen is spending time with. These parents may require the friends to spend time in the parent's home (especially if it is a dating relationship) before allowing the teenagers to spend time alone together. Authoritative parents may call or make arrangements to meet the parents of their teen's friends. Also, authoritative parents are aware of their teen's activities and require him to ask permission before going out or changing plans. Finally, these parents set limits on what is and is not acceptable, and make continued access to privileges contingent on following the rules that have been established.

Now, all this doesn't mean that authoritative parents never encounter conflict with their children and that their relationships with their children are problem free. Children of authoritative parents are still children and they are learning what behavior is and is not acceptable. Like all kids, they will challenge their parents as they learn the limits. In addition, authoritative parents are not one-hundred percent consistent in their parenting approach. Like any parent, they are human and will likely be permissive at times and authoritarian at other times.

A word of caution here: Inconsistency in parenting results in increased uncertainty by children in regard to their parents' expectations. When expectations are inconsistent, children are less able to predict whether or not specific behaviors are acceptable or will be effective in meeting their wants or needs. Such inconsistency tends to result in a decrease in positive behavior and an increase in problem behavior. You and your spouse need to be on the same page with (or come to an agreement on) as many parenting issues as possible.

Parenting Styles and Anger

The various parenting styles do influence and have an effect on children and their anger problems. **Authoritarian** parents express a more aggressive approach to parenting. They make decisions based on what they want with very little, if any, consideration given to the child's needs and wants. Thus, children parented in this fashion learn to behave in a similar aggressive and self-centered manner. That is, they are likely to take or do what they want with little or no consideration for others.

When a child of an authoritarian parent becomes angry and expresses anger at the parent by yelling, storming out, etc., the parent responds with anger over being treated with disrespect. Authoritarian parents have difficulty seeing the child's behavior as a reflection of emotions, skill level, and developmental stage. Instead, they take the child's behavior personally. This means, they believe that the child is acting this way to be disrespectful and that this disrespect is unacceptable and must end immediately. The parent's perspective is, "I am the parent. You will respect me."

Authoritarian parents may use force (grabbing the child) or overly harsh punishments (extended groundings, taking away all toys, selling gaming systems, physical discipline) in an attempt to control the child's behavior. Ultimately, what the child learns from the parents (via modeling) is that anger, physical force, and excessive negative consequences are acceptable when a person feels poorly treated or offended.

On the other end of the parenting spectrum, children raised with a **permissive** parenting style are likely to become angry and retaliate when their wants are not readily met. Children of permissive parents are accustomed to getting what they want when they want it. So when they don't get something they want on their timeline, they are likely to respond with anger. These kids have not yet developed the skills needed to delay gratification or appropriately cope with disappointment. As a result of what they don't know, they become angry.

Permissive parents do not want their children to be upset or experience disappointment. That's why these parents are likely to respond to their children's anger by getting or giving them what they want or by finding some other way to appease them. Ultimately, this teaches children that when they don't get what they want when they want it, anger will work to get it or something comparable – or possibly even something better.

Children raised with an **authoritative** parenting approach learn that their wants are sometimes met, while at other times they are not met. These kids learn there are limits and boundaries that build and protect healthy relationships. Authoritative parents may be better able to tolerate their child's upset. They don't necessarily take the upset and behavior personally because they understand that upset and disappointment are part of life. As a result, they model and promote problem solving, compromise, and fair enforcement of expectations.

These parents are better able to respond to their child's anger by delivering consequences in response to the child's behavior rather than out of their own anger. For young children who hit when angry, this might result in a time-out. For older children, it might mean extra chores. For a teen, it might result in a grounding from a specific privilege for a limited time. Ultimately, the child learns that anger does not produce a positive outcome; rather, it results in a negative consequence. Over time and with enough repetition, the child will figure out that anger expressed inappropriately doesn't work very well.

How to Change Your Parenting Style

If you have discovered that your parenting style tends to be more permissive or authoritarian and you want to change, there's good news. You can learn how to parent differently – and better. Here are some steps you can take to implement that change:

Take stock of how you parent.

Chances are you aren't one-hundred percent permissive or authoritarian in your parenting approach. Rather, you are probably more permissive regarding some issues and less permissive with others. The same is likely true if you tend to be more authoritarian in your parenting style. Take notice and determine where you tend to lean more heavily toward a particular parenting style. The key here is recognition so you know where and when you need to change your approach.

Start changing by doing something that's a bit easier for you, rather than something more difficult.

So, for example, if you tend to be a permissive parent and you know your eight-year old will throw an intense tantrum if you try to set a limit around clothing, then don't start there. Instead, it might be better to start with a different issue. So, you might begin to influence or shape your child's eating habits by modifying what you put in her lunch box. If the child is used to chips and a cookie, pick one and replace it with a piece of fruit or a container of yogurt. You can include the child in the process of choosing which healthier option she prefers. If she doesn't want to pick an option, let the child know you will pick it for her.

If you are a more authoritarian style of parent, look for an issue you can be less strict about. Perhaps clothing is a good place for you to start. The idea is to increase the child's involvement in decision making. So, you might start by choosing two outfits you approve of and allowing the child to make the final selection. To reduce the potential for conflict even more, you could pick out two tops and two bottoms that can be matched interchangeably. Begin at a place you are comfortable with and slowly introduce new situations and issues over time.

Praise your child's positive behavior and continue to take small steps toward your new parenting style.

For permissive parents, that means adding more issues and opportunities to increase parental involvement, while authoritarian parents should work to add more child involvement. Permissive parents should praise their child's patience, acceptance of their decisions, and cooperation when the child appropriately accepts increased involvement. Authoritarian parents should praise their child's decision making, maturity, and responsible behavior when making positive decisions. Let your children know how proud you are of them.

Notice your efforts and give yourself some credit.

Also, be patient; change takes time. Whether you have been parenting for five years or fifteen years, you have had lots of practice parenting the way you do. Changing how you approach parenting takes repetition, determination, and patience. Chances are when you are stressed, worried, or angry, you might slip back to the parenting style you've always used and are comfortable with. That's okay; no one is perfect. Just pay attention, expect setbacks, and anticipate and plan to parent differently in future challenging situations.

Learning to Become a Better Parent

There are several ways you can learn to parent more effectively. Reading this book (and others) is a great way to discover new parenting skills and strategies. Attending parenting classes, like Boys Town's Common Sense Parenting®, is another way to further improve your knowledge of and skills at parenting. Classes also give you the opportunity to interact with other parents whom you can talk and listen to, learn from, and share experiences with.

Health professionals are another good source of parenting information. Parents most often seek advice and direction about concerns with their child's behavioral and emotional functioning from their primary care providers, pediatricians, and family doctors. The health professionals who are specifically trained to assist parents with concerns like these are called behavioral pediatric psychologists. Psychologists and qualified mental health therapists strive to understand the child's current functioning and assist parents in learning how to facilitate positive change on a day-to-day basis.

As children age, parents typically get caught up in the "business" and busyness of life and often forget to make time to simply "be" or do things with their kids in loving and caring ways. The next section discusses some tried-and-true approaches to parenting children. We will revisit the fundamentals of parenting, including unconditional love and accepting, approving, and appreciating your child regardless of the nature and severity of his or her problems. When parents consistently love, accept, appreciate, and provide approval to their child over time, healing can take place with the child's anger problems (or any other problem) and with the parent-child relationship.

The following information is practical, positive, and easy-to-use, so you can take it from these pages and use it with your children in your home today. As always, if you don't find improvement after using these approaches consistently over time, you should consider taking a parenting class (see Parenting.org^SM for more information about Boys Town's Common Sense Parenting® classes) or visiting with a health professional.

Unconditional Love

No matter the type, severity, or number of problems your children might have, one of the best ways you can help them is to show them you love them unconditionally. There will be times when that's a lot easier said than done, because kids often choose to do and say things you don't like. Sometimes (more often than we as parents would care to admit), parents withhold expressions of love and affection from their children until they exhibit desired behaviors. When parents and children forge this kind of conditional relationship, positive change becomes particularly difficult to achieve.

Instead, children need to know they are inherently good and their parents love them. One way to do this is to say loving and caring things to them. Simple verbal interactions and statements can be potent signs of your love and affirmation. For example, you can say simple, easy things to your child like:

- "Good morning" when he wakes up.
- "Have a great day" before you leave for work.
- "Good bye" before she leaves the house for school or some other activity.
- "Tell me about your day" when your child gets home from school or you get home from work.
- "I love you" before bed (or anytime during the day!).

All these are examples of small, quick things you can say to express your unconditional love for your child.

You also can communicate your love with quiet acts of affection. For example, you can give your child a hug or kiss in the morning, before you or the child leaves for the day, upon arrival home, and before bed. These are all convenient, practical, and meaningful times to show physical forms of love and affection to your child. Other unspoken signs of affection include rubbing your child's back, stroking his hair, and holding her hand. These are all powerful expressions of love.

Simple gestures like these can take quite a bit of effort if you are not now in the habit of engaging in them. My clinical experience has shown that parents don't frequently engage in physical touch with their children, even after I encourage and prompt them so I can observe the interaction. If you are out of the habit or even if you think your child might not want you to, work to increase how often you touch your child in loving ways, then observe the positive changes that take place.

If your child is often angry and it's been a while since you've shown gestures of affection, start by offering brief, silent displays of affection (touch or rub your child's back, stroke her hair, offer a side hug or squeeze of the shoulders, etc.). Initially, your child may not return the affection and may even resist it. But, don't give up after one or two tries. Instead, be patient, persistent, and consistent so you can be the parent you want to be.

At first, you may need to balance what you want with what your child will allow regarding loving touch and verbal statements of affection. However, once your child knows you have no agenda other than to show your love, you can increase how much and how often you do and say loving things.

Let's go back to the example I discussed at the beginning of the book about my daughter who was often angry. When I made the decision to begin demonstrating unconditional love through physical gestures like hugs, her initial reaction was a stiff, straight-armed posture until I let go. Her expression wasn't exactly pleasant or welcoming either; it was more like, "Eww...stop it!" I also would smile at her and tell her I loved her at least a couple of times a day. And, I made sure to interact with her every morning by saying things like, "Good morning!" "How did you sleep?" "Have a great day." I made sure to do and say similar things at night before she went to bed, too. During all of this, I made sure to have no expectations about her giving me anything similar in return. I was hopeful my efforts would have a positive effect, but I didn't expect her to respond favorably or in kind during the moment. So that meant not criticizing her lack of positive expression or verbal response to me. Over time – and really not too long, just a few weeks – my daughter began to initiate hugs and other positive and affectionate verbal and physical interactions with me. And best of all, she seemed to become increasingly happy and less often angry.

It's important to be consistent and to continue with your loving words and gestures over time, even when you don't get them in return right away. It'll likely take a bit of time before you notice a difference in your child's responses to you and an improvement in angry behaviors. So hang in there; it'll be worth the effort in the long run.

The Three A's of Parenting

The head of my department at the Clinic, Dr. Pat Friman, teaches in his trainings to parents and professionals that people want and seek out **acceptance, approval,** and **appreciation.** All individuals no matter their age want to be accepted, and they want others, especially loved ones, to approve of and appreciate them for who they are and what they do. Children especially want, and more importantly **need,** to know and experience these things from their parents.

As a parent, I know how easy it is to get caught up in getting things done and feeling overwhelmed and stressed about all that's not yet accomplished. When I get home from work, I have to make an effort to interact with my children in ways where I'm not just quizzing and questioning them about their homework, grades, and chores. And it's hard to ignore the obvious messes around the house and tasks to be done. But I have come to realize I can get to all that later. Instead, it's extremely important for parents to just "be" with their children in loving and caring ways where they are free from conditions and interrogations. So, each day, I try to show acceptance, approval, and appreciation to my kids before I get down to the household business. Like you, if I don't make a concerted effort to do this, then all the other business issues of running a home will take over and the time I spend interacting with my children in loving ways will diminish and suffer.

I've also discovered my children need balance between the demands placed on them from school, home, friends, and extracurricular activities, and from the interactions and activities that hold no demands. Sitting with your children while they play video games, watch TV, or play on the computer are excellent ways to be present without placing any demands on them. I have been surprised at how much my sixteen-year-old son enjoys it when I watch him play video games and allow him to explain what is going on. He enjoys it even more when I actually play a game with him.

Children figure out pretty quickly when parents place demands on them every time they are in the same room. When this happens, children begin to avoid being around their parents. That's why it is so important for you to make a conscious effort to just "be" with your children. So play with them and their toys when they are young. Invite them to play cards, board games, go for walks, and make snow angels as they get older. With older children, have movie nights, go out to dinner, and watch their activities giving nothing but compliments afterward.

Parents need this same kind of balance regarding creating space in their lives for downtime and fun. When I get caught up in the demands of home, work, and all my other commitments, responsibilities, and tasks, I don't feel very effective as a parent and my children really don't respond well. When parents have balance in their lives with work and play, their children are happier, respond more positively to people and situations, and require less direction and redirection from their parents.

The three "A's" of parenting are excellent ways to help you get back to the fundamentals of parenting. And they give you the opportunity to just "be" with your children in loving and caring ways. Let's take a look at each one.

Acceptance

One way to think about acceptance is to always remember that your child is a gift from God. You readily accepted and were excited to bring your baby into the world. As a newborn, your child didn't have to do anything to earn your acceptance – it just happened naturally without any conditions. Today, your child's personality is still developing and evolving. His or her temperament is more obvious, and the child has learned many positive and negative behaviors. However, at the core, your child is still that same infant you so readily cherished and accepted at birth.

Accepting your child does not mean you approve of anger or the way he or she behaves when angry. Acceptance means you value your child as a human being, an individual, and as your child. Acceptance means taking responsibility and caring for your child, providing the basics of safety, food, shelter, and clothing, and advocating for the child's education, health care, development, and mental health. Children should not have to earn or work for any of these things. Parents are responsible for providing and caring for their children – doing so relays the message of acceptance.

It is important for you to tell and show your child this message of acceptance as often as possible. One powerful way to do this is to find and create opportunities to simply listen to your child. When children come home from school frustrated about an incident with friends, just take the time to **listen** to what they have to say. Don't try to fix the problem, ask questions about their actions, or give advice; instead, hear them out. While you may have good intentions or see the situation as an opportunity to teach a lesson, restrain from doing so. Instead, seize the moment as an opportunity to communicate acceptance. If needed, there will be plenty of time for teaching later. At that moment, just give your full attention and listen. You might even be surprised to hear that they handled the situation well or have a solid plan of action in mind.

When it comes to situations when your children are angry, it doesn't do any good to focus on whether or not they should be angry. The fact of the matter is that they are angry and are experiencing the emotion. There's nothing wrong with this, and it's important for you to accept that. It isn't helpful, for example, to tell a child that he shouldn't be angry or that it is wrong to be angry. The issue is not about your child experiencing the emotion of anger; rather, it is about how he goes about expressing or acting on that anger. So the sooner you accept the fact your child is experiencing anger, the better. That will then allow you to look for opportunities to teach skills when your child responds to anger in unhealthy and inappropriate ways.

Approval

Approval is not the same as acceptance. You can accept your child without communicating approval. Approval is about having and communicating a favorable opinion of your child to her. Parents communicate approval and disapproval in many ways. Smiles, pats on the back, and hugs are all nonverbal signs of approval. Nonverbal signs of disapproval include frowns, sighs, broken eye contact, and spankings. Verbal examples of approval include statements like "I am proud of you." "You did a great job!" "Way to go with your grades this quarter." "You played a great game!" "Way to work hard!" Verbal examples of disapproval include telling your child that she should have done something different or that what she did was wrong.

With approval, your challenge is to separate the child as a person from his actions. You can communicate approval of your child and disapproval of his actions in the same interaction. For example, you might say, "I am proud of you for being ready on time. It is still too cold out for shorts so please go put on some pants." Or, if your child is angry and shouting at you, you might, with a concerned expression, say, "I know you are angry. Think about your choices right now. Yelling is not helping." In both these examples, you are telling the child that you approve of him as a person but not his behavior.

To be able to do this, you must first get in touch with the approval you do feel for your child so you can then communicate it sincerely in your words or actions. A good way to do that is to reflect on (and even write out a list of) your child's positive qualities, then remind yourself of them when dealing with and addressing problem behavior.

Appreciation

Appreciation involves showing admiration and respect. Expressing admiration to your child requires a foundation of acceptance and approval. For example, let's say your child enjoys music, plays an instrument, and practices diligently every day. Here, you **accept** your child's interest in music, **approve** of her decision to play an instrument, and, ultimately, **admire** her dedication. When it comes to anger and your child learning to express it more assertively, you might express admiration for her effort, self control, and determination to manage herself better. This would be a powerful message of appreciation for how hard your child is working to better deal with anger.

Separating out acceptance, approval, and appreciation can be challenging. It's important to do that here so you can better identify what you are already doing well and continue doing it, and what you might not be doing well and work to do more of it. Remember, however, that children don't know the difference between the three A's and don't keep track of them. Instead, they experience the outcome of what you say and do – and what you don't say and do. You have a powerful effect on what your children think and feel regarding whether they are liked, loved, or even wanted.

How your child feels and thinks typically changes depending on what's going on at the moment. However, when things in life are neutral or it's a typical day, your child has an overall general opinion of whether you accept, approve of, and appreciate him or her. Your task is to take the actions needed to show your kids that you do indeed accept, approve of, and appreciate them.

The Angry Child and the Three A's of Parenting

It has been my clinical experience that youth who have problems related to anger generally feel they are not good enough, can't do anything right, and are not wanted. Often, their parents clearly communicate to me how concerned they are and how much they want to help, which is why they sought psychological services. And before coming to me, they have tried all sorts of other things and talked with lots of different people about their child – all because they care for and love that child. There is a disconnect or mismatch between what the parents say they feel to me (and others) and what their child perceives about how they feel about him or her.

This is why one of my main tasks with these kids and their parents is to help the parents find clear and effective ways to better communicate their acceptance, approval, and appreciation to their child. And, my other task is to help the child understand and see the ways the parents show the child these things. The goal is to get the child and parents in sync so when parents communicate the three A's, the child recognizes and understands what the parents mean.

For a younger child, parents are the primary source of acceptance, approval, and appreciation. From the child's perspective, if parents don't accept, approve of, and appreciate him, then nobody will. That's why it's so important for you to fill these needs for your children as early in life and as often as possible.

With older kids and teens, it may seem like they only want their peers' acceptance, approval, and appreciation – and of course they do. However, teens were once children whose parents were their primary source of the three A's, and teens still want and need that from you. Also, when parents continue to strongly relate acceptance, approval, and appreciation to teens, they won't depend solely on peers for these things.

Communicating acceptance, approval, and appreciation is one of your most important jobs as a parent, especially when you have a child with anger problems. These children need to know that you accept, approve of, and appreciate them for who they are, what they are interested in, and their personal qualities. Doing so helps these kids feel better about themselves, better understand that you love and want what's best for them, and be more open to your guidance and teaching.

CHAPTER 6

Catch Kids Being Good

"Catch kids being good." Many of you may have heard this phrase. While it's an excellent parenting approach, it can be challenging to use, especially with children who are difficult to parent or manage due to mood or behavioral problems like anger. Nevertheless, catching kids being good is the best place to start once you have followed through with the suggestions discussed in the previous chapter (delivering unconditional love, acceptance, approval, and appreciation).

With some children, it might seem that instances when they are being "good" do not happen often. My observation as a parent and psychologist is that this is rarely the case. It's more likely that adults simply do not notice the many moments when children are being good and doing the right things.

Depending on their age, kids do many things well that are overlooked by adults, including:

- Getting up and starting their day without disturbing anyone.
- Getting dressed when they get up.

- Sitting at the table nicely during mealtime and appropriately using their silverware when eating.

- Playing, watching TV, or reading without disturbing others.

- Asking permission to have a snack, engage in an activity, or go out with friends.

- Answering the phone appropriately and politely.

- Playing with their toys gently.

Now, not all children engage in these kinds of behaviors without being told to do so or without conflict all the time. But there are many everyday, positive behaviors that adults tend to overlook and fail to praise and reinforce.

It's just human nature to notice and react to children's misbehavior. So it's usually very clear to children that parents pay attention when they engage in problematic behavior. On the other hand, when children behave well, adults take the behavior for granted and overlook it. Ultimately, this means adults are missing opportunities to use praise that reinforces good or appropriate behaviors.

Adults don't always pay attention to kids' positive behaviors because they feel children should be expected to behave. So why praise them for only doing what's expected of them? Let's look at it this way: What if you were treated like that at work? No one notices that you come in every day, or rewards you for working hard and well. What effect would that have on your motivation to perform your job well in the future? Well, kids are no different.

Everyone wants to be noticed and commended for what they do well. When that happens, it lets people know what they do is appreciated and matters to others. Work environments that include recognition for jobs done well and positive employee behavior are much more conducive to high productivity and employee retention than are work environments filled with criticism and indifference. So, why should we expect children to be any different in this regard? We shouldn't. In the end, they are just like you in their desire for acceptance, approval, and appreciation.

If you want more of the positive behavior your child exhibits, you must notice, praise, and reward it in some fashion. I recently had a sixteen-year-old female client share with me that her father surprised her with her all-time favorite treat because he was impressed with some work she had done for a neighbor. This simple act by her father meant a great deal to her and increased the likelihood that she will choose to help others again in the future.

How to Catch Kids Being Good

Noticing and reacting with praise and gratitude is at the heart of what catching kids being good is all about. If you want appropriate and positive behaviors to continue, it's imperative you make the daily effort to watch your children and observe their behavior. When there is no problem situation going on, it's likely your children are engaging in positive behavior. For example, let's say your daughter and son are watching TV and they are getting along just fine. Or, your teen is quietly doing homework at his desk. These are great opportunities for praise that reinforces their positive behavior. You might say, "I like how you and your sister are enjoying TV together," or "Thanks for getting your homework done."

An area where you can increase your awareness and catch kids being good is in their compliance with instructions. Many of the children I see in Clinic are described by their parents as "noncompliant." That is, these kids don't do what they are told. They might ignore their parent's instructions, talk back, argue, or throw a tantrum instead of doing what is asked. These parents really notice these instances when their children do not follow instructions.

However, **all** children follow **some** instructions. With parents in Clinic, I often use the example instruction, "Come in for some ice cream," as an instruction they can give to a child and then praise (and hopefully reinforce) him for following the instruction. Children generally comply with instructions that involve activities they enjoy, like having a snack, playing outside, eating a meal, going out to eat or to a movie, or engaging in some recreational activity. Also, parents frequently prompt their children to say "please," "thank you," or "good bye," and children usually do as asked. When children comply with instructions like these, give them positive attention and praise for doing so. This can be one way to begin giving praise even to children who often struggle with following instructions.

As parents, we give many instructions to our children every day and to pay attention to all of them is almost impossible. To increase your awareness of your child's compliance with your instructions, choose a couple of fifteen- to thirty-minute time periods daily when you can focus your attention on the instructions you give and your child's response. When your child does what you ask, let her know you appreciate how well she followed your instruction. The more you do this consistently over time, the more compliance you'll see from kids with instruction following.

What to Do When You Catch Kids Being Good

Praising and reinforcing kids for being good and doing the right things can take a variety of forms. In the last chapter, we discussed physical touch and how well that works as a way to show kids your approval. So, remember to use physical touch often and in ways that work best for you and your child.

Verbal praise also is a great way to reinforce appropriate behavior. For example, if you see your child playing nicely with others, you might say, "You are playing together and sharing so nicely. Good job!" Or, you could simply stop by and pat your child on the back, as long as you have paired the two behaviors (physical touch and verbal praise) in the past so your child understands the connection.

Tangible rewards or activities are powerful ways to reinforce good behavior. For example, special treats or activities, like a bike ride with mom or having dad read a bedtime story, might be very reinforcing to your child. From a practical standpoint, however, parents can't deliver a tangible reward or activity for every positive or good behavior. It is more manageable to use touch and verbal praise most often and deliver tangible rewards for behaviors that the child is working on or ones that are particularly impressive to you or difficult for your child.

Here are four suggestions you can use to make your praise even more effective and powerful with your children when you notice them doing something good:

Show your approval.

Be enthusiastic. Make children feel good about what they did, and make them want to do it again. You can use words like, "Awesome," "Terrific," "Wow," "All right," "Wonderful," and "Fantastic." Throw in hugs, kisses, winks, smiles, a "thumbs up," a "high-five," clapping, or a pat on the back. Whatever words or actions you use, look at your child, be sincere, and let him or her know that you are happy about what happened.

Describe the positive behavior.

Specifically describe what you saw or heard so your child knows exactly what the praise is for and what behavior you want to see repeated. Use words your kids understand, and be brief and to the point. For example, say, "Thanks for taking care of your brother while I was gone. It makes me happy to know that I can depend on you like that."

Give a reason for using the behavior.

Giving a reason helps kids understand the connection

between what they do and what happens to them or others. Reasons are especially important with verbal praise because they usually spell out the benefits kids will receive as a result of a positive behavior. This encourages kids to use the behavior in the future. Reasons should be brief, appropriate for the child's age, and believable. For example, don't tell a seven-year-old that sharing his toys with a friend is important because it shows maturity. A seven-year-old won't get it. Instead, say "If you share your toys with your friends, they will probably share their toys with you."

Give a reward.

Occasionally, you may want to reward your child for a certain behavior, a big improvement, or for doing something special. Rewards can be big or small, but the size should fit the behavior you're trying to encourage.

One key to success is remembering to praise a positive behavior immediately after it occurs. This makes the connection between positive behaviors and praise stronger. Kids start thinking: "When I shared my toys, Mom noticed and told me I did a good job. I like that." If you're already using praise and aren't seeing any results, look at whether you're not praising enough, praising too much (not making your praise dependent on positive behavior), or praising the wrong behaviors.

Rewards vs. Bribes

Some parents think that rewarding children is really just bribing them to be good. There is a distinction between rewarding children for positive behavior and bribing them. Bribes involve giving children something they want of value **before** they do the desired behavior or do something wrong. Rewards are delivered **after** the good behavior is exhibited.

If you disagree with this distinction and have ever been paid for a job you've done well, then by your definition, you too have been bribed. Rewarding children for doing something after they have done it is no different than you and me receiving paychecks for the work we've done and the time we've put in at our jobs. So remember, as you catch your child being good spontaneously, give a reward only after the positive behaviors are demonstrated, and not before, as a way to get the child to use them more often.

When it comes to the child who is often angry, I encourage parents to be diligent about noticing, praising, and rewarding their child's behavior when he remains calm (or calmer than usual) in situations that typically produce an angry response. Also, I encourage them to do the same thing for acceptable behavior(s) once the child calms down and corrects his behavior. For example, parents described how their eight-year-old son became angry when he saw a shirt laid out for him to wear. He began yelling and refused to wear the shirt, demanding something else. His parents responded perfectly by instructing him to take a time-out for yelling and not following instructions. When the boy calmed down and was released from time-out, he respectfully and appropriately asked to wear a different shirt and offered a valid reason for his request. The parents said "No" and explained their response by saying if he had asked nicely right away, they would have said "Yes." The parents told me they responded this way because they didn't want the boy to get away with having argued and thrown a tantrum. I explained that their son didn't get away with anything because they delivered appropriate consequences for his problem behavior. What the parents wanted was exactly what their son finally did after he calmed down: to respectfully and appropriately ask to wear a different shirt. My suggestion to them for when this (or something similar to this) happens in the future was to continue with giving consequences for problem behaviors, but to also praise their son for making the request appropriately and grant it to him in order to reinforce his positive behavior. This will help him learn how to respond positively, while also reducing his arguing and tantrums. Obviously, this won't happen overnight; it will take time and be a gradual learning process.

So even though your child's initial response might be inappropriate, once he or she calms down, you might see appropriate behavior that you can notice, praise, and reward. That way, your child finds the good behavior valuable and is more likely to choose to use it again and again.

Attention Is Powerful

You might be thinking, "Why all the emphasis on positive attention?" The straightforward answer is because attention is powerful. All attention, whether positive or negative, is powerful to children.

A common "disciplinary strategy" parents mistakenly use involves verbal interactions like reprimands, redirection, scolding, lectures, warnings, and other threats. The content of these verbal exchanges is unpleasant, negative, critical, and admonishing in nature. Parents might think children will change their behavior in order to avoid making their parents angry. And, parents might **intend** these interactions to be punishment for the problem behavior. In reality, these kinds of negative, angry verbal interactions end up reinforcing the child's behavior. Why? Because humans desire stimulation and attention. People, kids especially, don't like being isolated or ignored. That's why the worst punishment in the correction system is solitary confinement – people do not like to be isolated from others, movement, and things.

Now, what does this have to do with parents scolding and lecturing children? Well, if you aren't catching children being good and instead are only catching their problem behaviors, you are delivering attention to children only for their problem behaviors and not their positive behaviors. So, children learn if they want your attention, a sure-fire way to get it is to do something wrong. Therefore, when you ignore good behavior, you are punishing it, and when you reprimand problem behavior, you are likely reinforcing it – exactly the opposite of what you want to do.

Verbal reprimands, lectures, and angry responses to kids are seldom effective strategies for decreasing or punishing problem behavior. Chapter 3 pointed out that children learn by doing a behavior and seeing what happens, and that the more potent the response is to what happens the more effective it is in helping children learn. Ultimately, children can endure reprimands and lectures because, in their experience, these kinds of consequences lack potency and power. Children might be inconvenienced briefly, but they also have likely avoided or escaped something unpleasant or gotten what they wanted in the end. In addition, they have received all the attention and stimulation the interaction provided from a reinforcement perspective.

So, it's important for parents to keep their focus on catching children being good. Ideally, you should notice and praise five positive behaviors to every problem behavior you address or correct. That means after addressing or correcting a misbehavior you should try to find five things to compliment or praise before addressing another problem behavior. For example, let's say your teenage daughter was late getting up for school and you had to go to her room and say, "You overslept. You're going to be late if you don't get up right now." Your daughter gets up and quickly moves through her morning routine, and she ends up catching the bus on time. Here, the problem behavior you address is your daughter's failure to get up on time. After that, it's important to switch your focus to finding five positive behaviors to praise. These could include your daughter getting dressed quickly, looking nice and presentable, cleaning up her breakfast dishes, remembering to brush her teeth, being polite, and being ready on time. As these (or other) positive behaviors take place, stop and praise your daughter for them.

This ratio of praising five positive behaviors to every one negative behavior you address or correct also applies to problem behaviors that come up other than the original issue. For example, if your daughter snapped at her little brother on the way to the kitchen for breakfast, you should find five more positive behaviors to acknowledge and praise before she leaves – in addition to the five for oversleeping.

Now, this might seem like a lot of work and it can be in the beginning. But, it is well worth the effort! Give it a try and see how your child or teen responds. As you catch your child being good more often, you'll find that both of you are more positive around each other. That's when you can start reaping the additional benefits of you and your child being happier and having a better, more positive relationship.

So, give praise try! Catch your children being good – and do so often. Look for the many positive things they do each day and let them know you notice and appreciate them.

CHAPTER 7

SEt a GOOD EXaMPLE

Parents are their children's primary teachers, and everything parents do or do not do serves to teach their children. In Clinic, parents often say to me, "My child isn't learning anything," as we discuss their responses to their child's behavior. What they really mean is their kids aren't learning what the parents want the kids to learn. The fact, however, is that children are always learning – and the vast majority of what they learn comes from what parents do and say.

So, how do parents teach? In many different ways, including:

- By modeling or example.
- By what they pay attention to and what they ignore.
- By what they specifically teach their children to do.
- By what they allow their children to do and the limits they set.

Each of these is discussed throughout this book. In this chapter, we will focus on modeling and how parents can use it to teach kids better, more appropriate ways to behave when they are angry.

Walk the Talk

Parents model how and how not to manage anger on a regular basis. We've already established that anger is a naturally occurring emotion that cannot be avoided, and that it's triggered by all kinds of circumstances throughout the day. If the reality is that you will get angry, the goal then becomes how to handle anger in ways that can positively influence what your children learn.

The tricky part for parents who manage their anger really well (they remain calm, cool, and collected) is that the child might not realize how angry parents really are and how well they are managing their anger. The child might think the parents aren't angry at all or aren't nearly as angry as the child gets. In these instances, it's important for parents to actively communicate through words (or a conversation) that they are indeed angry and that their words will not match their tone and expression when they are managing anger well.

When parents don't manage anger well (they yell, become aggressive, throw things, slam doors, swear, etc.), it's obvious to the child they are angry. It is also obvious the parents aren't managing their anger well. In order to manage anger well and become better examples for their kids, these parents have to learn to remain calm when they get angry.

Be a Better Role Model When Angry

Let's take a look at six strategies you can use to manage anger better:

Take an inventory.

This means looking for examples when you manage (or have managed) anger well, then asking yourself questions like: What factors contributed to my behavior? Who was present? Did who was present make a difference in my behavior? Do I remain calm at work but not at home (or vice versa)? Do I remain calm in front of my boss, neighbors, relatives, and friends? Do I remain calm in public places? The purpose here is to try to figure out what factors serve as limits for your behavior when you're angry.

During the times you've managed your anger well, think about and evaluate why you chose to handle anger in appropriate ways.

Ask yourself questions like: Did I handle anger well because I didn't want to embarrass myself? Was it because I didn't want to get fired or wanted to avoid an argument? Did I want others to think of me as responsible? See if there is anything you can use from these situations and your evaluation of them that can help you in other situations where you are more likely to let your anger control you, rather than you controlling your anger.

Think about and assess situations where you are likely to become angry and not handle things well.

As you reflect on these situations, ask yourself: Is the issue or situation really that big of a deal? Did it serve me well to become angry? What did not handling anger well cost me in this instance? The answers to these questions will likely depend on who was present and what the outcome of the situation was. For example, you might determine that you are not likely to handle anger well if you are pulled over by a police officer for speeding. Think about what would happen if you argued and lost your temper with the police officer. The result would likely be a ticket and fine instead of a warning. Next, think about what your behavior would teach your child if he was present in the car with you. You would have taught him to be disrespectful when angry toward authority figures and to show it in ways that lead to unpleasant and negative results. This type of analysis can help you prepare for and better deal with difficult situations that might come up in the future.

Pay attention for a couple of days to how you act (what you do and say and what you don't do and say) when you are angry or frustrated.

Ask yourself questions like: What kind of behaviors am I teaching my child to use when angry? Is this how I want my child to behave when angry or frustrated? If the answer to the second question is "Yes," continue with what you are doing. If the answer is "No," make a decision to change what you are doing and a commitment to work on handling anger in better ways.

Decide how you would like to express yourself better when you are angry.

Then, think of practice situations and visualize exactly how you would prefer to act (what you would say and do) in situations that typically make you angry. If necessary, practice these situations with your spouse, a friend, or a relative.

Let your child know you are working to manage your anger better.

Apologize if you have mistreated your child (yelled, slapped, hit, name called, swore, etc.) when you've been angry. Let your child know you behaved poorly and will do your best to act differently in the future. Then, make the commitment to do so. Your child will believe – and learn from – you when she sees you working at it and acting differently in the future.

"Do as I say and not as I do" doesn't work well in parenting and won't help you effectively teach your children different, better ways to behave. The truth is children do as they see and not as they hear. That means they need role models like you who act in positive and healthy ways when upset, angry, and frustrated. So, save your breath; instead, let your children see you manage your own anger well by taking a deep breath and expressing it calmly. When you do, your actions will speak volumes!

CHAPTER 8

CONSEQUENCES WORK, SO USE THEM

Parents often think of consequences as negative or as punishment. Actually, consequences are anything – positive or negative – that occurs following a behavior. There are two types of consequences. **Reinforcers** are consequences that increase the likelihood a child will repeat a behavior. Consequences that decrease the likelihood a child will repeat a behavior are called **punishers.**

In Chapter 3, we established that children learn by doing and seeing (experiencing) what happens. The "what happens" are the consequences. By definition, children want reinforcing consequences. That is, they will engage in behaviors that will get them consequences they want. Also by definition, children want to avoid punishing consequences. That means they will avoid behaviors that result in consequences they don't want.

When it comes to teaching children how to manage their anger well and express it appropriately, consequences always play a role in what children learn. Parents can use consequences strategically to influence their child's expression of anger. At the most basic level, parents must make sure they aren't unintentionally reinforcing children for their inappropriate responses when angry (tantrums). At the same time, parents need to guard against unintentionally punishing children for managing anger well. Here are some examples of how these situations can happen:

Child Behavior	Parent Response	Consequence
Child tantrums when parent says "No" to candy or toy at the store.	Parent gives in and angrily buys the object for the child.	Child gets preferred item.
Parent tells a child to do a task and he yells, "You can't tell me what to do!"	Parent walks out of the room, and child doesn't do the task.	Child avoids doing what he doesn't want to do and can now do what he wants.
Teen comes home an hour after curfew. Parents ground daughter for one week. Teen shouts at parents and storms out of the room.	Two days later, parents let teen go out with friends.	Teen is not really grounded.
Parents question teen about poor grades. Teen yells at his parents that they are too strict.	Parents stop asking their son about his grades.	Teen is not held accountable for grades.
Parents place a child in time-out for misbehavior.	While in time-out, parents reprimand the child for crying and yelling.	Child is not actually in time-out because parents are still paying attention to the child.
Parent reminds teen to put away dishes. Teen yells, "I'm tired from practice! You do it!"	The parent puts away the dishes.	Teen avoids chore and does what he wants.

Some other examples that might be less obvious, yet still reinforce angry behaviors are:

Child Behavior	Parent Response	Consequence
Child dumps milk out of cup and cries that she wants juice.	Parent gives the child juice and reprimands her for wasting milk.	Child gets juice.
Teen complains and argues when parent tells him it is time to turn off his cell phone.	Parent gives the teen ten more minutes and walks away.	Teen gets to his use cell phone longer.

These examples might not appear to you to be reinforcers, meaning they increase the likelihood the child will repeat the behavior, because the examples involve yelling, lectures, and other harsh responses by parents. However, these consequences hold reinforcing power because they allow children to have what they want or avoid what they don't want. So, even though the parent's reprimands, redirection, and other harsh responses might be unpleasant to the child, getting candy or a toy, getting more time on the cell phone, and avoiding putting away dishes are more reinforcing than the parents' responses are punishing. Ultimately, this results in the child's angry behavior being reinforced and an increase in the likelihood it will happen again.

Use Consequences That Work

Consequences work when parents use the right ones and use them in the right ways. There are more effective ways parents can respond and deliver consequences so children are taught how to better manage anger and express it more appropriately. The first step involves making sure the angry behaviors and outbursts don't let children get what they want.

Let's take a look at each of the previous examples and see how parents might better respond and use consequences that are more effective.

Child Behavior	Parent Response	Consequence
Child tantrums because parent said "No" to candy or toy at the store.	Parent ignores the tantrum, saying nothing to the child.	Child does not get the desired item.
Parent tells a child to do a task and he yells, "You can't tell me what to do!"	Parent waits expectantly for the child to complete the task.	Child does the task.
Teen comes home an hour after curfew. Parents ground daughter for one week. Teen shouts at parents and storms out of the room.	Parents don't allow teen to have access to her privileges for one week.	Teen is actually grounded.
Parents question teen about poor grades. Teen yells at his parents that they are too strict.	Parents monitor grades independently of the teen or with the teen.	Teen is held accountable for grades.
Parents place a child in time-out for misbehavior.	Parents implement time-out effectively, by having no interaction with child until he is sitting quietly.	Child stays in time-out until he is calm.
Parent reminds teen to put away dishes. Teen yells, "I'm tired from practice! You do it!"	Parent waits expectantly for teen to put away dishes.	Teen has to do the task.

Child Behavior	Parent Response	Consequence
Child dumps milk out of cup and cries that she wants juice.	Parent silently refills cup with water and says, "No dumping. Now you get water."	Child gets water and not milk or juice.
Teen complains and argues when his parent tells him it is time to turn off his cell phone.	Parent waits expectantly for teen to turn off his cell phone.	Teen turns off cell phone on time as asked.

For many parents, the most challenging part of these kinds of interactions is remaining calm when their child becomes angry. Of course you might get frustrated or even angry, but it's important for you to manage your anger well. Even though you might feel angry on the inside, you can still work to appear calm on the outside and interact with your child in a cool and collected manner. Remember, you want your child to learn to do this, too, so it's up to you to set the example and model the desired behavior.

Another important feature of using consequences correctly is letting children fully experience them. Your role is to deliver ones you realistically can and will enforce. Otherwise, you aren't really delivering consequences; you are simply issuing warnings and threats. For example, grounding a child for thirty days is nearly impossible to enforce. Also, when your child is grounded, so are you. A more effective strategy to use is "task-based grounding." This involves requiring your child to complete one or more extra tasks that take approximately twenty to thirty minutes to complete, and the child is grounded from all privileges until the tasks are complete. If the child avoids the chore(s) for two days, she is grounded from all privileges for two days. If she does the task(s) right away, the grounding ends right away. The challenge for parents with this strategy is to avoid nagging the child to do the chore. The parent's focus should be on making sure the child does not access privileges until the tasks are done. That means you have to learn to be all right with however long the child ends up being grounded, because in essence the child is really grounding herself.

Parents have far more power at their disposal than they realize. You are the gatekeeper of nearly all, if not all, of your child's privileges. To help you fully grasp all the privileges you control, one strategy is to make a written list of all of the privileges your child has or would like to have. Since you are the keeper of all these privileges, you can give them out or take them back based on your child's behavior.

Some of the more common privileges parents write down include the following:

- Watching TV, DVDs, and movies.
- Using the computer, Internet, cell phone, iPod or MP3 player, and video games.
- Having fiends over or going out with them.

  In reality, there are many, many more, including:

- Having and using makeup, curling irons, flat irons, and nail polish.
- Stopping at a convenience store for a soda.
- Accessing soda pop, chips, deserts, or candy at home.
- Purchasing name brand clothes.

Also, some privileges are more meaningful to your child than others. The best way to find this out is to watch and see what the child likes to do and prefers most. This allows you to better determine what you can use as effective reinforcers and punishers.

Children and teens want what they want. And, they will work to get what they want when they have to. If kids don't have to work for their privileges, they won't. If they can throw tantrums, yell, and argue to get their privileges, they will.

Parents should let their children know what privileges they can access when they manage anger well. Also, when they don't manage anger well, children should know they won't have access to some, and in some instances all, of their privileges.

Let's look at a real-life example of how consequences can help with anger problems. A twelve-year-old boy I was counseling had to appropriately manage his anger each day to access the family's video gaming system. Managing his anger meant no swearing, no aggression, and no yelling or screaming. Some days, he did really well and earned access to the games, while other days he lost it as a consequence for not managing his anger. The challenge for his parents was to follow through and stick with the plan and consequence. Sometimes, if he got angry in the morning but turned his behavior around later in the day, they would let him play on the gaming system. However, this tended to backfire as the boy would again have problems managing his anger the following day. So, we worked together and agreed that the boy had to go a full day managing his anger appropriately in order to use the system. This meant the parents had to stick to the plan and consequence. They did and the boy's ability to manage his anger improved. In addition, the parents and I worked on several other strategies with consequences to help the boy successfully learn to control his anger even better.

Consequences are most effective when they are delivered immediately and fit the severity of the behavior. In addition, consequences should be age-appropriate. For younger children, negative consequences like time-out or loss of a privilege (watching TV, playing outside, using the computer, etc.) should be shorter in duration than what you use with older kids. This gives younger children more opportunities to learn appropriate behaviors, and allows them to learn desired behaviors more quickly.

For older children, consequences can be longer in duration, and they can be even longer for teenagers. For example, if a teen is able to calmly accept and follow the rules regarding cell phone use, she can have and use her cell phone. However, if she becomes angry and belligerent about cell phone rules (or about some other issue involving her cell phone), she forfeits access to her phone (which is a privilege, not a right) for twenty-four hours.

Parents can do the same thing when a younger child talks back, yells, or throws a tantrum when told it's time to turn off the computer, video game, or TV to do homework, finish a chore, or go to bed. She can lose access to these privileges, but it should be for an amount of time that's age-appropriate. Fifteen to thirty minutes is plenty for young children (ages five to seven), while the rest of the evening (one to two hours) is more appropriate for older kids. If the resistance and misbehavior comes at bedtime, the consequence will have to be delayed until the following day. Although not ideal in terms of being immediate, it is better than no consequence at all.

Parents tend to deliver more severe negative consequences when they are angry. Ideally, parents would learn to deliver consequences that help teach their children how to behave, what to do, and what not to do. However, when parents discipline out of anger, the consequences tend to be more severe and less practical. When they calm down, many parents realize they have overreacted and simply let the consequence slide altogether. When this pattern is repeated time after time, children learn they don't have to take their parents seriously. They also learn the behavior the parent overreacted to is actually okay or acceptable to engage in because they never really receive a negative consequence for it.

Consequences should be planned out ahead of time so everyone – especially the child – knows what to expect when behavior is appropriate or inappropriate. The most effective positive consequences are things that children like or want. Negative consequences that work best are things that kids don't like or want to avoid. For example, seven-year-old Henry likes to play cards with Mom. So, if Henry does something nice for his sister, he knows he can earn fifteen minutes of extra time playing cards with Mom. On the other hand, Henry doesn't like the chore of helping clean the dishes. So, he knows if he talks back to Dad, he will earn two extra times to help with the dishes.

Remember that consequences can help change behaviors kids use in response to anger. It's also essential to understand that consequences involving physical punishment or words or actions that demean, embarrass, or otherwise diminish a child's self-worth and confidence are not appropriate or effective in the long run. Using consequences should be part of a strategy that teaches children new behaviors in a positive manner.

CHAPTER 9

LISTEN TO AND TALK WITH YOUR CHILDREN

One of the challenges parents face when teaching children how to manage anger well is hearing and understanding what children are really saying with their words and actions. Children may direct anger at their parents by saying things like, "I hate you!"; "You are so unfair!"; or "You are overreacting." When this happens, it is important for you to remember that your children are expressing emotional upset in the safest way they know how at that moment, and that they don't always mean what they say. At times, adults do this, too. When we become angry and express it poorly, it can be easier to blame it on someone else or on the circumstances instead of taking responsibility for our actions. If adults do this, it's not surprising that kids do too.

Older children and adolescents typically know when they have done something wrong. But that doesn't mean they want or plan to be held accountable for their actions. There's a good chance they did what they did with the hope and expectation that they wouldn't get in trouble. When they get caught and are held accountable – meaning they receive a negative consequence – their next agenda is to escape the consequence. And, if talking, whining, yelling, complaining, and blaming have worked to get them out of negative consequences in the past, they will certainly use those behaviors again.

Sometimes kids will counter with aggressive behavior toward their parents or themselves. Anger and aggression toward parents may include claims from kids that parents are unfair, are ruining the kids' lives, don't understand them, and never listen to them. Some teens might even take their aggression out on themselves by engaging in self-harm that is meant to punish, but not seriously injure, themselves. This kind of self-harm can include superficial cuts or burns.

Whether kids take verbal jabs at you or engage in physical actions like self-harm or self-injury, these kinds of behaviors in response to anger are inappropriate and harmful. Your job is to remain calm and teach your children new, healthy, and assertive ways to express themselves when they are angry. Let's talk about how you can go about doing that.

Listen to Your Kids

The best thing you can do when children are angry is to simply **listen** to them. And I mean really listen. That means working hard to hear what they are saying about their lives. For example, they might communicate they are unhappy with their appearance, friends, lack of friends, grades, clothes, athletic ability, etc. Many kids, especially teenagers, don't see the same attractive, talented person in the mirror that parents and others see in front of them.

When I hear children or teenagers be self-critical, my first impulse is to disagree with them or try to convince them how beautiful, bright, and talented they are. But, I've discovered this is not a very productive response. In fact, it seems to make the child or teenager resist hearing the compliments, along with whatever helpful advice I might have to offer. What seems to be more effective is simply listening to what they have to say.

What do I mean by listening? Allow children to do most of the talking. It's okay for there to be some silences between their statements and yours; that's just a normal part of give and take in conversations. Instead of doing a bunch of talking, let kids know you want to listen to what they have to say by offering statements of support like these:

- "That sounds like it was tough to hear."
- "How discouraging."
- "You sound like you are really disappointed in your appearance."
- "It sounds like you are worried about being left out by your friends if you have to stop texting now."

Giving lectures on what real friends are like, how attractive the child is, or how smart he would be if he only applied himself more are not helpful when emotions are running high. These kinds of conversations are perfectly fine to have when parents and children are calm and there's not much else going on, but they are unhelpful and unproductive in the heat of the moment.

Take mental notes of your child's or teen's comments when angry and follow up on them later when you have time and your child is calm. When it comes to young children (preschool and elementary age), I usually suggest following up on strong statements made during an angry outburst at a time when children are engaged in a preferred activity. For example, let's say your preschool child yelled, "I hate you!" or "You don't love me!" Reacting to these statements in the moment isn't helpful and will likely serve to distract you from the core issue that initially triggered your child's angry outburst. Instead, wait a bit and interrupt your child when she is playing or watching TV and say something like, "I need to talk to you for a minute. You said something this morning that I want to check in with you about. You said you hated me. Is that really how you feel?" The child will very likely say something like, "No, I just said that because I was mad." At that point, you can teach and say, "Okay. What I would like you to work on is saying something else when you are angry like, 'I am really mad right now.' It's not okay to say hurtful things just because you are mad."

In the heat of the moment, some children might make self-harm statements like, "I wish I was dead" or "I just want to die." Here, you can tell them those kind of statements are not acceptable and if they say something like that again, you will have to take the child to the ER (emergency room) to make sure he or she is safe.

With adolescents, staying calm and listening when they are angry serves several purposes, including:

- You are modeling calm behavior for your teen to use during stressful and upsetting times.

- You can evaluate how your teen is handling a situation compared to how he handled previous situations and note any progress made.

- Your reaction does not escalate the situation; rather, it helps to lessen and calm heated emotions.

- When the teen reflects on the situation later (and he will), he will primarily remember his voice because the child did the vast majority of the talking (yelling, screaming). Thus, the child won't have much to blame on you. If you responded to your teen's anger by blaming, accusing, or belittling him, then the teen will focus on your behavior and not his own.

So, stay calm and give simple statements that direct your teen to express his anger more assertively: "Please lower your voice." "Take a step back." "Think about what you are saying." This way, when your teen is thinking about and mentally replaying what happened later, your voice will be remembered as one of reason and calm, while his voice is the one that is angry, hurtful, and aggressive.

- Finally and most importantly, your actions will show your teen how much you care for and love him even when he is angry.

Talk with Your Kids

Think about how much time you've spent talking with your child (or children) over the last couple of days. Disregard interactions like telling your child what to do, giving instructions, reminders about chores, redirecting problem behavior, and other parental commands and requests. Now, how much quality conversation is left over? By that I mean how much time did you spend talking with your child about her day, what's going on at school and with her friends, video games she is playing, books your child is reading, or music she is listening to? When put this way, many parents admit they don't have much meaningful conversation with their children at these levels.

Conversation is the cornerstone of strong relationships in a family. Talking is the main way parents and children communicate. It's how most of the teaching and learning that takes place in a family occurs. Topics of conversation may range from trivial to profound; it doesn't matter. What matters is that parents and children are sharing information about themselves and what's going on in their lives. Human beings need to feel like they belong, like they are connected to the people who are closest to them. Talking to someone fulfills that need. And families with strong communication skills are better able to solve problems, make decisions, and get along.

If you and your kids can comfortably talk to each other, you have a great gift; don't lose it. If you have trouble getting conversations started, or you don't know what to talk about, start slowly, use the suggestions presented in this section, and work on getting better as you go along.

When it comes to talking with children, the main challenge often is getting them to talk to you. The trap many parents fall into is asking too many questions. Questions are usually a good way to get a conversation started. But, the problem arises when a question is asked, the child gives a one-word response, and the parent follows up with another question. This pattern can repeat itself until you can't think of any more questions or the child's brief responses punish you out of asking any more questions. Either way, the result is the same: communication stalls. This frustrates, concerns, and discourages parents because they are not getting much information and feel like the child doesn't want to talk to or share with them.

Put yourself in your child's shoes. When getting rapid-fire questions, one after the other, the child grows frustrated and irritated. After all, no one likes being "interrogated" or "grilled." So, the child simply tries to escape being questioned by giving one-word answers.

There are many ways to establish and maintain good communication with your child. How you go about doing that varies with your child's age. The conversation strategies you would use with toddlers are much different than what you would use with older children and teens. The remainder of this chapter discusses these differences and how to effectively communicate with toddlers, school-aged children, and teenagers.

Toddlers

As soon as children start talking, parents are ready with questions. "Who is this?" The toddler responds, "Mama." "Who is that?" The child answers, "Dada." "What is this?" The child says, "Ball." "Where are your eyes?" The youngsters points to her eyes. The list of possible questions is practically endless.

What parents don't realize is every time they ask their toddler a question, they are placing a demand on him to perform. And, they are teaching him how important it is to get the answer right. Parents do need to teach their child many things, and they are the child's first and most frequent teachers. So, questions are necessary for teaching. But, there needs to be a balance between demands to perform and opportunities for the child to learn that he is a capable, competent, and worthy individual without having to perform.

Children can make good choices, solve problems, demonstrate patience, and follow rules all on their own. However, the young child's real job is to play. This is how they learn and demonstrate all kinds of new skills. That's why play is an excellent time for parents to interact and talk with their toddlers and younger children. That doesn't mean asking questions about what they are doing or building, or instructing them on how to do something better. Rather, parents should simply watch and describe what they see. Play also provides many opportunities for parents to praise their child's behavior.

There are several names for this kind of interaction style with your child: "the child's game," "time-in," and "child-directed interaction." Regardless of what it is called, you are following the child's lead rather than leading or directing the child. You are providing positive, focused attention on your child's spontaneous good behavior.

While this may sound simple, it is often very difficult for parents to do. We want to ask questions, tell our children what to do, and solve their problems. But, when providing positive, focused attention, we must resist these temptations. In place of that, you can do the following:

- **Watch** what your child is doing.
- **Describe** to the child what he or she is doing – "You are putting a blue block on the red block."
- **Praise** the child's behavior – "I like how gently you are playing with the blocks."
- Optional: Use touch as a **reward** for your child's positive behavior – rub the child's back.

Research has repeatedly demonstrated that just five minutes of this kind of positive, focused attention each day can make a huge difference in children's behavior.

When using this approach, parents are modeling speech for children; teaching them through attention what behavior is acceptable; teaching children concepts like colors, shapes, positions, and counting by describing and labeling what you see; increasing the time children are on-task; promoting imitation for children; and demonstrating sharing and taking turns. Also, by letting your child figure out how to build something or make something work on his own during play, you are promoting self-confidence as he successfully solves problems. Finally, as you describe and praise your child for staying calm and working hard, you are promoting and teaching self-control, how to cope with frustration, and how to be persistent.

It is okay to help when your child asks for it. Be sure to help just enough to get him going again, then back off and let the child figure things out. If your child isn't asking for help, simply continue to watch, describe, and praise while he engages in trying to figure out the challenge.

I see how parents struggle to do this when children attempt to put together a difficult puzzle I have in my office. Parents want so badly to help by telling their child exactly where to put the puzzle pieces. And, when the child puts a piece in the wrong place, they really want to show how to fix it. It takes every ounce of effort (and a little prompting from me) to get parents to resist this tendency and let their child figure it out. Instead, we talk about how they can better help by watching, describing what they see their child doing, and praising the child's patience, determination, and willingness to keep trying.

Often, parents are surprised at how long their child perseveres at solving the puzzle and how calmly he or she goes about doing it. And, there is nothing like the joy and pride children feel and show when they figure the puzzle out independently.

During your child's play, there are instances when you can allow yourself to get involved, including:

- When your child invites you to play. Go ahead and join in but keep the focus on your child and let him or her drive the activity.

- When your child asks you a question, go ahead and answer it.

When situations like these occur, remember to keep your involvement brief and get back to watching, describing, and praising as soon as possible.

Use this kind of interaction strategy with toddlers and young children as much as possible. You'll find they really enjoy it when you interact with them in this way. Also, you'll likely find this strategy challenging because it's a new way of doing things, but stick with it and you'll discover how effective it is.

Talking with toddlers and young children after they have done something wrong is important, too. The biggest challenge here is to teach in ways they can understand and learn from. At younger ages, fewer words are more effective. Younger children track and comprehend about one word for each year of their age. So, for example, if you are disciplining your two-year old, use two words; for your three-year old, use three words; and so on. What can you say in so few words? A lot really. With a two-year old, you can say, "No hitting." Then, place the child in time-out. For a three-year old, you could say, "No hitting. Time-out." Then place the child in time-out.

When it comes to noncompliance with young children, it's okay to repeat your instruction one time with a warning of a negative consequence. If the child complies, praise him or her; if the child doesn't comply, deliver the consequence you stated in the warning. Don't change your voice tone or raise your voice, and don't repeat the warning. Just calmly follow through. For example, let's say you instructed your child, Sam, to put on his socks but he keeps playing with his blocks. You might say, "Sam, put on your socks or I will put away your blocks for thirty minutes." When he continues to play with his blocks, you could say, "Sam, I am putting away your blocks (as you pick them up) because you didn't follow instructions. Put on your socks." When he complies and puts on his socks, you could say, "Good job listening, Sam. You will be able to play with your blocks again in thirty minutes." If Sam cries, complains, or tries to bargain, stay calm, follow through, and resist arguing or lecturing. (We will talk much more about what to do when you child doesn't comply or loses self-control in later chapters.)

School-Age Children

It is also a challenge to avoid the question and one-word answer trap with older children. To do this, I encourage parents to pay attention to the type of questions they ask their children. This is important because you want to avoid asking questions that can easily be answered with one word.

There are two basic types of questions: open-ended questions and closed-ended questions. Closed-ended questions can be answered with a single word. For example, "Did you have a good day?" can be easily answered with a "Yes" or "No." Or, "How was your day?" can be answered with "Okay" or "Fine." When starting a conversation, closed-ended questions are fine but don't exclusively use them throughout a conversation with your child or you may just get a string of one-word answers in response.

Open-ended questions are great to use with children because they require more than a one-word response and promote information sharing. Examples of open-ended question include:

- "What was the best part of your day?"
- "What was something that made you laugh today?"
- "What did you and your friends do at recess today?"
- "What was the hardest work you had to do today at school?"

Open-ended questions like these are better conversation starters. They allow your child to open up and share. Once your child starts talking, use the strategy just presented (watch, describe, and praise) to keep the conversation moving along.

Be careful not to punish your child for sharing information. For example, let's say your child tells you he got angry at recess and the teacher made him stand by the wall. Most parents are tempted to start asking questions about what happened, tell their child how disappointed they are that he got in trouble, or tell the child what he should have done. Responses like these make the child feel that he has been punished twice, and he won't want to keep talking and sharing with you.

A different, more effective response includes active listening, which might go like this: "It sounds like you were pretty angry during recess and made a good choice to stand by the wall when the teacher told you to." This kind of response helps to keep the conversation going and allows the child to feel comfortable sharing with you what he learned or thought of the incident. For example, the child might respond by saying something like, "I get in trouble every time I play with Jared. Tomorrow, I'm going to play with someone else." You can then say, "That sounds like a good idea. I'll be interested in hearing how it works out for you."

If your child says something that concerns you or makes you think he might continue getting into trouble, try to keep the conversation going without telling him what to do just yet. For example, if he blames the teacher or another student and talks about getting even, keep using your active listening skills and ask opened-ended questions like, "What do you think might happen if you tell all the other children not to play with Jared?" "Anything else?" This way, you can keep the conversation moving forward and help the child think through what he has learned and is thinking about doing. If the child describes behavior that is inappropriate and not allowed, calmly let him know you will be following up with his teacher, and if he chooses to do the problem behavior again, he will earn a negative consequence from you.

You might be wondering what to do at home when your child gets in trouble at school. As a parent and psychologist, I often recommend letting school personnel manage behavior problems at school. So, in the previous example, the child lost recess time as a negative consequence for his problem behavior. There is probably nothing more you need to do regarding consequences at home. But, it is important to praise the child for accepting the teacher's consequence, and let him know you hope he will make a better decision next time so he doesn't get in trouble.

Children who come to the Clinic with school behavior problems may require strategies that include positive and negative consequences in school **and** at home for their school-day behavior. Even with these children, I am careful to make sure they are not being doubly punished for one behavior, and I work with the parents to find ways to reinforce positive behavior. If your child is really struggling with behavior problems at school and what school personnel are doing doesn't seem to be working, you should seek additional services that might be helpful (talk to the school counselor or a mental health professional).

When your child does something wrong or inappropriate at home, it's important that you interrupt the behavior as soon as you can and deliver a negative consequence in a calm, matter-of-fact manner. Then, describe what the child did that was not okay and why. You don't need to lecture, and you really don't want to engage in an argument. For example, let's say your daughter is watching a TV show you have said is off-limits. As you shut off the TV, you might say, "Jenny, as you know, you aren't allowed to watch this show. Since you were watching it, you are not allowed to watch TV for the rest of the day." Jenny will probably complain by saying things like, "I just turned on the TV and wasn't actually watching the show." "There wasn't anything else on." "This rule is unfair!" When this happens, stay calm and don't engage in an argument. Simply say, "Jenny, you broke the rule and the consequence stands. You will have to find something else to do."

Teens

How to get teenagers to talk and open up more is a common difficulty and source of frustration for parents. Recently, my teenage son has started answering some questions by saying, "Meh." When I asked what that meant, he said, "Okay or mediocre." As a parent, I find his response annoying and would prefer that it go away. But, I remind myself that he is at least saying something, and that it is up to me to continue looking for ways to draw more words out of him.

For many of today's parents, having time to talk with their teenager is a challenge. School, extracurricular activities, jobs, friends, and homework take up much of the teen's day, leaving little time for you and your child to talk and catch up. And, once teens begin driving, you even lose that "car time" when you could chat on the way to taking them someplace. That's why with teenagers, it's especially important that you take advantage of any snippets of time you have to visit with them.

An excellent place to start is at family meals when everyone is sitting around the table. During this time, you can talk about upcoming events, recent social activities, current movies, local and world news, or humorous family memories. Also, you could share interesting information about your day that might prompt your teen to ask you questions.

When you don't have time to eat or spend time together as a family, check in with your teen in other ways. You might call or text, or check in when the teen is doing homework or before going to bed. Find a least a few minutes each day to chat with your teen – a little time talking is better than no conversation at all.

When your teen does share information, use the same strategies discussed in the previous section, including:

- Ask open-ended questions.

- Avoid disciplining or telling your teen what to do when the information shared with you is troubling.

- Keep the conversation going with active listening skills so you can learn more about what your teen is thinking and the decisions he or she is making.

- Praise your teen for good choices and decisions.

- Briefly inform or remind your teen of the possible consequences (positive and negative) of his or her actions.

When your teen has done something wrong, like missing curfew or going out without permission, you need to talk about the misbehavior. You can effectively do that by:

- Letting your teen know you need to talk and find a time when that works for both of you.

- When you get together, calmly telling your teen what was wrong, what the consequences are, and what should be done differently next time.

- Explaining you are disappointed in your teen's behavior and providing a rationale for why the behavior is a problem.

Let's look at an example of a teen missing curfew. Here, you might say, "Sarah, you came home twenty minutes past your curfew last night. When you are late, your father and I get concerned that something bad might have happened to you and we worry. Since you were late, you will not be allowed to go out tonight, so let your friends know you won't be joining them. We are disappointed you didn't pay closer attention to the time and make your curfew. We want to be able to trust you and coming home on time really does matter."

Talking with your children and teens is important. When you do, you communicate interest, caring, and love. You also learn what they are thinking, what their interests are, what is going on in their lives, and where they are in their developmental journey toward maturity. So, pay attention to how often you talk with your kids and look for opportunities to do more of it in ways discussed in this chapter. Changing the way you communicate with your children is not always easy. But in the long run, the payoff is worth the effort!

CHAPTER 10

WHERE IS YOUR LINE IN THE SAND?

Try to remember being a teenager. How much confidence and self-worth did you have? While I don't necessarily think it is tougher to be a teenager today, it is very different. In this age of advanced technology, there are so many more ways for kids to be cruel and to be in touch or out of touch, including cell phones, text messages, instant messages, social networking websites, and others. Children need to know their parents are there no matter what to listen to them, love them, and teach them. That doesn't mean children can take out their anger on their parents. It does mean parents should help establish boundaries and rules for kids to express anger.

How far has your child or teenager gone in terms of his or her behavior when angry? Has she hit you? Has he called you vulgar names? Does your toddler spit on or growl at you? Is there shoving, arm grabbing, or cocked fists? If children repeatedly engage in these types of aggressive behaviors when angry with you, they have discovered and learned they can. That is, nothing in the way of significant negative consequences have occurred to change or stop the behaviors. Instead, these angry and aggressive behaviors are working, so children won't change or stop them.

So, the next set of questions to ask yourself are: "How am I responding to these angry behaviors?" Am I backing off, yelling, or threatening my child instead of remaining calm and teaching? Am I following through with consequences for negative behavior? Begin to think about and develop boundaries regarding acceptable and unacceptable behavior for when your child is angry.

Draw a Line in the Sand

When I work with children and teens who express anger in harmful ways toward their parents, I ask the parents what their limits are – in other words, what is their "line in the sand." Often, they aren't clear on their limits, so I encourage them to talk and come up with some decisions they can live with. For example, we might develop and define simple household rules the parents want their children to follow. I encourage the children and teens to be thinking about the rules, too. Then, we write up the rules in a "to do list" format. Each rule states what the parents want and what the child or teen **is** to do, rather than what the child is **not** supposed to do.

Common rules can include:

- follow instructions when told the first time
- accept "No" for an answer
- ask permission before using something that belongs to someone else
- keep hands and feet to self
- tell the truth

Also, when it is helpful in terms of clarifying a rule's intent, you can put the behaviors kids are not supposed to do next to the rule in parentheses. For example, you might list the rule as "use appropriate language and talk respectfully" but follow that with "no swearing, yelling, arguing, or name-calling" in parentheses.

I encourage parents to post the rules and monitor their kids' adherence to the rules. If children break a rule, parents are encouraged to deliver an immediate consequence without giving any warnings for violations.

I also advise parents and inform children that if they become physically aggressive and threatening toward their parents, parents are to call the police. However, before the children are informed of this strategy, I make sure parents will follow through with it. Some parents might need convincing. When this happens, I use these rationales with them:

- We don't want parents and children getting into physical fights and having someone get hurt.

- Should a parent become physical with their child and the child is injured, Child Protective Services might get involved.

- Children need to know this kind of behavior is serious, and police involvement clearly communicates that message.

After we have that discussion, chances are good parents are willing to follow through with a call to police when needed. Some kids will test their parents to see if they really will call the police. So, I encourage parents to contact their local police department or, if they know someone on the police force, to call that person and explain what they are doing ahead of time. This way, when the police are called to the house, they know what to expect and so do the parents. Police will let the child know it is not okay to be aggressive toward the parents and that if the aggressive behavior continues, the police might have to remove the child from the home.

Up to this point, I have been talking about the most extreme angry and aggressive behaviors. Parents also should draw lines in the sand for less severe behavior and develop and communicate consequences to kids. What parents choose to deal with first depends on what the behavior looks like when the child is angry. For example, if the child is physically aggressive toward the parents, eliminating hitting, kicking, biting, and similar behaviors is the first step. If the child makes only verbal threats, then eliminating verbal threats is the first step. Parents first need to figure out what they want and expect so they can communicate their expectations clearly to their children.

Secondly, your child has to learn to express anger differently. We have talked about teaching through the use of consequences – and that information applies here as well. However, there are ways you can teach and use consequences at various times so your child learns new and better ways to respond when angry. For example, when you proactively teach your child how to respond differently when angry, you are establishing ahead of time what the consequences will be, both positive and negative. This approach works well with school-age and older children, but it's not effective or appropriate for toddlers. With this age group, parents should focus on "catching them being good" and praising and reinforcing their positive behavior. When toddlers exhibit anger in inappropriate or unacceptable ways, parents can set limits by enforcing immediate brief consequences like "time-out." For older kids, you can teach new positive behaviors they can use in place of negative behavior. These teaching techniques – teaching proactively, using praise, correcting misbehavior, and using time-out – will be discussed in detail in the following chapters.

What You Can Do

To determine your "lines in the sand," you and your spouse or partner should think about, discuss, and come to an agreement on your limits and boundaries. To do this, you can use the following questions during your discussion to help it along:

- What rules do you want your children to follow?

- How severe does a problem behavior have to be for you to deliver a negative consequence?

- What will it take for you to know you need more help with your child or teen?

These questions are a good starting point and will help you begin to clarify and make clear your limits. Once you've come to an agreement on these issues, write down what you decide. Then, sit down with your children and review the list with them. This way, everyone is clear about what behavior is acceptable and not acceptable and what consequences will be.

CHAPTER 11

TEACH AHEAD OF TIME

Parents usually know what their child is doing that they do not like or disapprove of. As a parent, I am quick to notice undone chores, belongings left lying around, and my children or teens watching TV, reading, or playing video games while I am making dinner or doing laundry. In Clinic, parents often express frustration with children being disrespectful, not listening, arguing, talking back, etc. What parents are frequently less aware of are the situations that lead to these problem behaviors and specifically what they would like their child or teen to do instead.

Teaching children and teens what you want or expect them to do is important. I have talked about how children and teens learn and the various ways parents teach. This chapter is about directly teaching or talking to your children about the specific behaviors you want them to demonstrate in various situations. It is important to keep in mind that you also teach by how you act in similar situations. Children and teens are more likely to do what you do rather than what you tell them to do. So, if what you do matches what you say, you are going to get further faster when it comes to teaching and changing behavior.

Parents typically realize they want their child or teen to use some other behavior after he or she is engaged in the problem behavior. The child has already learned the negative behavior. So in most cases, we are working to change negative or inappropriate behavior into positive, healthy behavior. This teaching and learning process takes time and requires that the child engage in the new behavior over and over, and realize that it can work to the child's advantage. However, if the problem behavior continues to work better for the child or teen, it will be more difficult to replace with new behavior.

Teaching children and teens exactly what you expect them to do in certain situations involves figuring out what behavior you expect, telling the child or teen your expectations, and practicing the behavior. This is not as simple as it sounds, but it also doesn't have to be overly complicated. You do need to spend the time thinking about your expectations and defining them so you can explain them clearly.

Once you've decided on and explained the alternative behavior, it is important to practice, practice, practice. Do this at neutral times (when the child is in a positive frame of mind and is not doing another preferred activity) and make the practice fun. Treat it like you would when teaching your child to drive a car in an empty parking lot. Empty parking lots provide plenty of space, with no lanes or other cars or traffic signs to deal with. All the person is doing is getting used to driving the car. You can do the same thing with practicing a behavior or skill. You don't have to deal with things that can complicate your teaching, like strong negative emotions, genuine desires being denied, or having to complete non-preferred tasks. Have some fun while your child simply begins to learn the steps of the new behavior.

Practice gives your child or teen the opportunity to learn and successfully use new skills and actions. And, it creates an experience where using the behavior is paired with pleasant feelings and thoughts. Let's look at a couple of examples of how all this works.

Two common situations that result in problem behavior are when parents tell children or teens to do a task, give an instruction, or tell them "No." The first step is to determine exactly what you want your child to do in each situation. Let's start with the skill of "Accepting 'No.'" Parents want the child to look at them and then just say "okay" when receiving a "No" answer without arguing or whining. Next, you would explain those steps to the child and say that you expect the child to follow them. Finally, you would practice or role play various situations where the child should use the new skill.

In Clinic, I recommend that children ask for something silly or things they know the parent will say "No" to. This makes practice fun and eliminates the risk of children becoming angry when denied something they really want. In effect, this is how to create an "empty parking lot." Examples of fun or silly requests are:

- (For young children) "Can I drive the car home?"
- "Can I have a thousand dollars?"
- "Can I get a baby elephant?"

Following the request, you say "No." You can offer a rationale or reason if you think it would help. The expectation is for the child to look at you and say "Okay." You then give feedback and praise (enthusiastically!) for using the skill steps correctly. For example, you might say, "Great job! You looked at me, said 'Okay,' and stayed calm." Keep in mind that praise is more potent when it is sincere, enthusiastic, and includes some form of touch ("high five," pat on the head, rub on the back).

The skill of "Following Instructions" can be taught similarly. The only difference involves the number of steps to the skill. The skill typically includes four steps: look at the person, say "Okay," do the task, and check back. Again, make the practice fun by giving a silly instruction. For example, you might ask the child to give you a hug, do three jumping jacks, and then stand on one foot. When the child uses all the steps correctly, you give specific feedback and praise the child.

Let's talk a bit more about feedback; its importance in your teaching cannot be overstated. Parents often say things like "good job" and "stop that" as a way of giving feedback to kids. These statements are better than nothing, but they aren't nearly as powerful as giving kids specific feedback about what they did wrong and what to do next time. Remember, you are teaching a new behavior so kids will need specific feedback to learn the skill. For example, if you give general feedback for an instruction ("Thanks for putting the dog outside"), children won't think about using the correct steps to the skill (look at you, say "Okay," and check back) because the message they receive is that the only important thing was doing the task.

Ultimately, you get to decide what's important and what you want your child to learn. If you are really only interested in the task getting done, then teach that by focusing on completing the task when told. Practice it and make it fun. And, tailor your feedback so it's focused on just doing the task the child was instructed to do. If you want some other combination of steps, teach exactly what you want, and reinforce the steps by describing them in your praise and feedback. ("Thanks for saying, 'Okay,' putting the dog outside, and then checking back with me. You did a great job!")

It's a good idea to remind children about the skill when they are faced with real-life situations, especially when they are first learning the skill or when it's a new or difficult situation. For example, if your daughter asks to go to a friend's house and the answer is going to be "No," you can remind her of the steps to accepting "No" answers. You might say, "Remember, the steps for accepting 'No' are to look at me and say 'Okay.'" Then, you can give the "No" answer after the prompt.

When children engage in behavior parents expect, they should pay attention and let the child know they noticed. You can even get silly if you want – fall down as though fainting.

Just show your child how pleased you are that she actually engaged in the behaviors you expect. Praise is powerful so use it often!

Over time, as your child increasingly and correctly uses the skills and expected behaviors, you can decrease the use of practice and reminders.

Proactive Teaching with Kids Behaving Aggressively

Boys Town has developed and trained tens of thousands of parents in a more formal teaching method called **Proactive Teaching.** It is designed to help parents teach children and teens appropriate behaviors they can use in future situations before they actually occur.

Let's look at how teaching ahead of time can help you change your child's aggressive behaviors. Children and teens who have difficulty managing their anger often engage in a combination of problem behaviors when they get angry. They might yell, hit, throw or break things, swear, stomp off, cry, call out names, make hurtful comments, slam doors, etc. Your first step is to think about what your child does. The next time your child gets angry, pay closer attention and notice all the behaviors he exhibits. Next, list the behaviors the child engages in from least to most problematic, bothersome, or dangerous. The final step is to determine what you want the child to do when he is angry, and what those behaviors look like.

The strategy discussed here helps you to achieve the desired behavior you want your child to exhibit, and involves gradually eliminating the current negative behaviors your child exhibits. The strategy works in the opposite direction of the teaching strategy described in the previous section. With the strategy discussed here, you start with what the child already does when he is angry and gradually shape that aggressive response into an assertive one instead.

125

Begin by working with your child to define what behavior(s) will be eliminated first, second, third, and so on. As the child successfully eliminates each behavior, praise the child's progress and reward it. Keep in mind this procedure gives the child permission to do the other more problematic or bothersome behaviors for now. Ultimately, all of the problem behaviors will be eliminated and replaced with an assertive response.

Many parents want to get rid of physical aggression toward others first; however, it's up to you to determine what behavior you find most problematic and want to eliminate first. A priority is to keep the child and others safe. If safety is not an issue, then your preference as a parent paired with what the child can reasonably do can guide your decision making.

Let's look at an example of this strategy with a child who exhibits aggression by hitting, yelling, using foul language, stomping off, and crying. The strategy begins with determining the first behavior to eliminate, which would be the child not using physical aggression toward others when angry. So, the child would be informed that when he gets angry, he is not allowed to hit anyone or anything. This means he can still yell, use foul language, stomp off, and cry. And, as long as the child doesn't hit, shove, push, or use any other physically aggressive behavior, he earns positive consequences.

With this approach, school-age children can earn stickers or smiley faces on a calendar each day they go without using any physical aggression toward others. The stickers or smiley faces act as effective and immediate reinforcers for younger children. For older children or teens, parents might consider using money (one dollar a day) or access to more time with specific privileges (computer, video games, curfew, etc.). Parents and children should agree on and set goals for these behaviors and rewards ahead of time so children can reach time-based goals.

When using this kind of teaching approach with children and teens, it's important for parents to pay attention to and apply some key steps, including:

1. **Determine how often the child becomes aggressive.** If it's daily, the first goal may be for the child to go three days without being physically aggressive. If it is weekly, you might set ten days as the first goal. When something like stickers are being used, determine how many stickers the child must earn during that time period before getting a reward. Once the first time-based goal is achieved, set a new time-based goal that is slightly longer.

2. **Determine ahead of time what the reward will be if the child achieves the goal.** Children don't need huge prizes that cost lots of money. Instead, simply going out for ice cream, on a bike ride with a parent, or having a friend sleep over might suffice. To determine the most effective and appropriate rewards, it's important to ask what your child wants to earn.

3. **Hold the child accountable for problem behavior when he gets angry.** For example, if your son gets angry and starts swinging his fists, you can send him to his room or to time-out until he is calm. Or, you can give him an extra chore. You should continue to intervene with that problem behavior. Change your expectations as his behavior progresses and focus on moving him toward the ultimate goal. So, when he gets angry and can resist engaging in physically aggressive behavior, deliver positive feedback and the agreed-upon reward. Ignore other problem behavior(s) that may still be occurring (like swearing or yelling). Focus on the absence of aggression (no hitting). It might sound something like this, "Connor, when you became angry earlier today you did a great job keeping your hands to yourself. Because you did that, you have earned extra TV time like we agreed. I am proud of you."

4. **Once the child consistently demonstrates being able to get angry and not engage in physically aggressive behavior, set a new behavior goal.** To continue with the previous example, you might decide with your child that

he can yell, stomp, and cry when angry. However, he may not use foul language or be physically aggressive toward anyone or anything. That means when he gets angry, yelling, stomping, and crying are considered acceptable for now. The child doesn't earn any severe consequences as long as he doesn't use any physically aggressive behavior and he doesn't swear. When the child successfully does this, he earns an agreed-upon reward (more computer time for an older child or a sticker or smiley face to put on the calendar for a younger child). If the targeted behaviors are exhibited (in this example, aggression and/or swearing), the child earns a negative consequence (an extra chore, earlier curfew, or reduced TV time for an older child, time-out for a younger child). Once this behavior goal is met, a new time-based behavior goal is set, along with the rewards the child can earn.

5. **Repeat this process until the child can express anger in an assertive manner.**

How long this process takes depends on several factors and is different for different children. Children who get angry every day will get more practice and experience with positive and negative consequences, depending on their behavior. As long as parents respond and teach consistently, the child who engages in aggressive behavior daily will likely learn the new positive behaviors sooner than the child who gets angry once a week. How often the child gets angry also impacts how long it takes to set new behavior goals. A good rule of thumb is you want to see the child manage anger without using the targeted behavior more than one time before you move on to setting a new goal.

Also, be aware that it's not unusual for children and teens to start to eliminate other problem behaviors you have not targeted. For example, if they can't swear, they may stop yelling, too.

Finally, be sure to talk with children or teens about what they can do when they are angry to replace the negative behaviors you are trying to help them eliminate. For example, if your child tends to hit when angry, you might suggest that she punch a pillow in her bedroom or do some type of physical exercise instead. Or, if the child tends to swear, you might encourage her to talk about her anger without swearing. Conversations about alternative positive behaviors are best held when you talk about goals and rewards that the child or teen is working toward.

As you make progress and set new goals, it's a good idea to talk with children about what seems to be working the best to help them calm down or manage their behavior when angry and what isn't working. That way, you can make adjustments as needed.

Keep in mind that it's unreasonable to expect your child to express anger appropriately and with more self-control than you do. If you struggle to stay calm, work to better manage your words, voice tone and volume, expression, and actions when angry. If your struggles continue, keep working to improve your behavior or lower expectations for your child so they match the expectations you have set for yourself.

Having different expectations for you and your child sends a couple of mixed messages you likely don't want to send, including:

- When you are really angry, anything goes.
- It is okay for adults to be aggressive, use foul language, or say hurtful things when angry.

These two messages are in opposition to everything you are working hard to accomplish with your child. Finally, if managing your own anger is difficult, at the very least, don't let your child see you acting inappropriately when angry.

Example of Proactive Teaching

Justin and Sam are friends, but they don't always get along. In the past, the two ten-year-olds have had some pretty good arguments and fights over who gets to play on the swing first or who is ahead in one of their driveway basketball games. Recently, Justin's dad and Sam's dad decided to try something new: Before their sons get together to play, each dad talks with his son about how the boys are expected to behave when they get angry at each other. Specifically, the dads teach their sons how to act if the boys have a disagreement. Both dads tell their sons how they can settle their differences calmly, without yelling or fighting, and that if they can't do that, they are to come home. When the boys play without yelling or fighting, they both get to do something fun with their dads. If the boys yell or fight, they have to help clean the house. In the two weeks since the teaching started, the boys have had only one fight.

• • •

The dads in the example are using a type of proactive teaching that works well with kids. In fact, you've probably already used a form of it with your child. Think about the times you talked with your teen about safe driving practices or what to do if their friends decided to drink or smoke while they were hanging out. You probably told your younger child how to safely cross the street, call 911, and be careful near a hot stove. In all these instances, you were trying to prevent problems by telling your child what to do before encountering that specific situation. That is Proactive Teaching.

Proactive Teaching is describing to a child what to do in a future situation and practicing ahead of time. It combines clear messages about what behavior is expected, kid-related reasons for using the behavior, and practice. Though it can be used in many areas, it is an especially good tool for helping kids learn assertive ways to respond in situations when they get angry and have resorted to aggressive or other problem behaviors in the past. It's best to use Proactive Teaching when your child is calm and attentive, not when problem behavior is occurring or when he or she is already upset.

Here are the three steps to Proactive Teaching. Each step is followed by an example of what it would sound like if Justin's dad (from the earlier example) was using it with Justin.

1. Describe the behavior you would like to see.

"Justin, I want to talk with you for a minute before you go over to Sam's house to play. When you and Sam disagree, I want you to try not to argue. If you both want to be first then try to work out a way to take turns. If you start to get mad and you can't calm yourself down, come home right away so you don't get into a fight with Sam."

2. Give a reason.

"If you can work things out without fighting, you'll have more fun playing. And you won't have to come home sooner than you want."

3. Practice.

"Okay, before you go, let's practice. Pretend I'm Sam and I just told you that I want the ball first when we play basketball. Tell me what could you say?" (Justin says it's okay if Sam takes the ball first.) "Great! That's the way to prevent an argument. And you can take the ball first for the next game. Now go have fun."

Children won't always have the right answer or know what they should do. In this example, Justin might not know what he should say when he and Sam both want the basketball. In this situation,

Justin's dad could handle the practice step this way:

"Okay, before you go, let's practice. Pretend I'm Sam and I just told you that I want the ball first when we play basketball. Tell me what could you say?" (Justin says he doesn't know.) "That's all right. I'll help you. What about letting Sam have the ball first and then taking turns after that? Would that be better than arguing?" (Justin nods.) "Okay. Tell me again what you should say?" (Justin says he could let Sam have the ball first.) "There you go! You've got it! And you can take the ball first for the next game. Now go have fun."

Proactive Teaching only works if you remember to use it. When you do a lot of teaching, you not only frequently remind the child about the expected behavior but also provide more opportunities to practice it.

Remember, children learn by doing and experiencing what happens. The "what happens" in Proactive Teaching is not as powerful as the "what happens" in real-life situations, but Proactive Teaching is something that helps to increase the likelihood your child will use the new behavior in the real-life situation. So don't get discouraged if your child doesn't use the positive behavior right away. You may have to practice lots of times before your child learns what you are trying to teach and begins to use it consistently. Don't expect perfection right away. It took your child some time to learn the negative behaviors you're trying to change, and it will take some time to learn the new behaviors you are teaching.

CHAPTER 12

"I'M SO ANGRY I COULD...!" NOW WHat?

Situations involving anger can get serious and out of hand when adults and kids fail to manage their emotions and instead allow their emotions to manage them. That's why adults and children need calming strategies to use when angry. These strategies give you and your kids positive and productive ways to pause and think about how to best work through emotionally charged situations.

There are a variety of strategies adults, teens, and children can try and use. And, "trying out" strategies to discover which one(s) works best for you and your child is extremely helpful. After all, different calming strategies work differently for each person. In this chapter, we will introduce and discuss some of the various techniques adults and children can use to help themselves calm down when angry.

Calming Strategies

There are **thinking** strategies and **physical** strategies people can use to cool down. For example, counting to ten is a thinking strategy, while deep breathing is a physical strategy.

There are many other strategies to try, but these two are popular because they are effective, easy to use, and appropriate for a wide range of ages. Let's take a closer look at each one.

Counting to Ten

Counting to ten targets a person's thoughts and attempts to "buy" a little time before the individual responds. If you are counting to ten, you aren't thinking about whatever it is that's making you angry. And if you aren't thinking about what's making you angry, you can begin to calm down. As you do, you are better able to respond in more productive and less-severe ways, and ultimately handle the situation better.

Deep Breathing

This technique is recommended to counter the body's natural physiological response that takes place when someone is upset. When a person (at any age) perceives a threat, the body's nervous system activates the "fight or flight" response. This means the person's heart and breathing rates increase, and blood flow is shifted to major muscle groups and away from non-essential organ functions. Why does this happen? So the person can "fight" off the threat or run away ("flight") from it.

The problem is that not all perceived threats are actual threats. For example, a parent confronts her teenage son for missing curfew and he responds as though he's been threatened. Here, the teenager's physiological response supports his perception of a threat and the "fight or flight" response kicks in. Even if the son quickly realizes there is no real threat, it will still take his body several minutes to calm down and reverse the nervous system response. Deep breathing can assist the boy in doing this because it helps to increase the amount of oxygen in the blood and calm the nervous system.

It has been my experience that children and adults expect deep breathing to work immediately, and when it doesn't, they think deep breathing doesn't work at all. In reality, deep breathing does work; it just takes a bit of time.

The other advantage to deep breathing is that it is the opposite of what people tend to do when they are upset. The "fight or flight" response just described may also trigger rapid breathing. Rapid breathing tends to be shallow and limits the intake of oxygen, making less available to the body. Deep breathing has the opposite effect on the body.

I have learned that people really do not know how to deep breathe. I describe it as "belly breathing." When teaching children how to belly breathe, I break it down into three steps:

1. Breathe in slowly through your nose to the count of four.
2. Hold your breath to the count of four.
3. Exhale slowly through your mouth to the count of four.

I often encourage children to place their hands on their belly to feel their breath move in and out. They also can try lying on their tummies when practicing at home to feel the air move in and out.

Like any other skill, deep breathing takes practice. And, it is always best to practice at neutral times so that when children are angry, they will be more likely to remember to use deep breathing to calm down.

The only way calming strategies work is if the child or adult actually wants to calm down, and then willingly implements a strategy to do so. If the person's real effort with using the strategy reveals little positive effect, then a new strategy is warranted. For example, if counting to ten is insufficient to distract and help your daughter to calm down, then doing mental math problems, like simple addition or multiplication problems, might prove to be more productive and effective. Ultimately, the goal of any strategy is for a child to calm down before reacting; however, it's essential to desire to do this for the strategy to really work.

Calming Strategies for Children and Teens

Children and teens often need incentives to help create the necessary desire for them to "want to" calm down when angry. Parents will need to develop and provide appropriate, effective rewards for their kids that encourage them to learn and use calming strategies. Also, when situations that provoke anger occur with you and your child, it's imperative that you react in appropriate ways that demonstrate maturity and self-control. So if you are upset and need to use a calming strategy yourself, do it! This is a powerful lesson for your child.

The table below lists some of the more common and effective physical and thinking strategies that work well for children and teens. Keep in mind that none of them will work if kids don't want to use them. Children are more likely to use a strategy if they help choose it and make it their own.

Once you and your child have decided on some strategies to try, you can encourage their use when you see your child becoming agitated or angry. Then, reinforce the child for using the strategy.

Physical Strategies	Thinking Strategies
Doing sit ups	Counting to ten
Punching a pillow or punching bag	Doing mental math problems
Running	Writing in a journal
Walking	Drawing
Doing push ups	Listening to music
Deep breathing	Reading

Using Charts

For younger children and children with developmental disabilities, parents can make the practice of using calming strategies more concrete by using a chart to help children know when and which strategies to use. For example, one family I worked with created the chart shown on page 138.

Let's take a closer look at the chart's components and how they work:

- The faces on the left hand side of the chart range from "enraged" to "happy." This helps the child learn to identify how frustrated or angry she is in a more concrete way. Pictures are easier for children to understand than words.

- The descriptions next to the faces help the child learn how changes in her mood go along with changes in behavior.

- The thermometer down the middle of the chart is used to help the child visualize how angry she is in a more concrete way – from not angry (bottom of thermometer) to as angry as possible (top of thermometer).

- Intervention and calming strategies are listed on the right side of the chart to remind the child what to do or what will happen when she becomes increasingly angry and does not take steps to calm down.

Now, let's go over how this chart worked. As you move up and down the chart, the faces and behaviors change to match the intensity of the emotion, and the corresponding calming or intervention strategy also changes to fit the emotions and behaviors. For this child, the face at the top of the chart represented "enraged" – or a ten out of ten on an anger scale. When the child reached this level of anger, the strategy was for the parents to "call the police." So, when the child became angry, her parents would pull out the chart and show her the faces, along with the corresponding "heat index" on the thermometer, that represented how angry she looked to them. Then, the parents pointed at and read to the child the corresponding calming strategy to use for that particular level and intensity of anger. The goal here was for the child to calm down before she ever reached the point where the police had to be called.

Emotion – Behavior		Intervention or Calming Strategy
Enraged Physically out of control		Parents call the police for assistance.
Very Angry Threatening to hurt others		Parents take you to your bedroom.
Angry Slamming, stomping, throwing		Parents tell you to go to your bedroom.
Irritated Arguing		Go to your bedroom.
Frustrated Talking back		Walk away.
Upset Complaining/ whining		Take a deep Breath.
Disappointed Feeling tearful or questioning		Tell yourself, "Stay calm. It's okay."
Happy		Do your thing with permission.

Ultimately for this child, the use of the chart resulted in her learning to recognize when she was agitated or angry. Eventually she was able to recognize her anger without her parents having to point it out. Once she was able to do that, she then learned to initiate using the strategies that helped her to calm down and avoid more severe consequences.

This is a good example of how you can use a visual aid to help a younger child learn. Try this with your children to see if it is effective and beneficial in teaching them to calm down when angry.

Using Time-Out with Toddlers

Teaching to toddlers is a whole different ballgame than teaching to older children and teens. In order to learn best, toddlers need immediate consequences in response to their behavior. They do not have the cognitive ability to connect delayed consequences to earlier behavior(s), even if you explain it to them.

The simplest and most effective strategy parents can use to teach toddlers how to calm down is time-out. However, it must be done correctly – and in my experience, many well-meaning parents don't actually do time-out correctly. When done properly, time-out helps children learn that screaming, spitting, biting, growling, and other angry and aggressive behaviors are not okay and don't serve them well.

Time-out is a teaching technique. This means children learn what behaviors are not okay because they result in going to time-out, and what behaviors are okay because they do not result in going to time-out. Children also have to learn how to do time-out. That is, they have to learn that they will be in time-out until they are able to sit or stand quietly.

Time-out teaches children how to calm themselves down or learn to "self-quiet." Children must become upset in order to learn how to calm down or self-quiet. Self-quieting is a skill just like many others and learning how to do it requires practice.

Time-out allows children to express themselves in any way they choose while in time-out without engagement from the adults around them. Over time children learn that none of their disruptive behavior gets them anything they want from others. They also learn that calming themselves and sitting quietly works to get them out of time-out. As a result, they learn to self-quiet, and they learn to complete time-out. Ultimately, they learn to avoid engaging in the behaviors that result in time-out and to behave in positive ways that keep them out of time-out.

Time-out Guidelines

Dr. Pat Friman, Director of Boys Town's Center for Behavioral Health, has written and spoken extensively about time-out and how to go about doing it correctly. In this section, we'll review Dr. Friman's time-out guidelines.

Time-out is a way of disciplining your child for problem behavior without raising your hand or your voice. Time-out involves removing your child from the good stuff in life, for a small amount of time, immediately following problem behavior. Time-out for children is similar to penalties used for hockey players. When a hockey player has misbehaved on the ice, he is required to go to the penalty area for two minutes. The referee does not scream at, threaten, or hit the player. He merely blows the whistle and points to the penalty area. During the penalty time, the player is not allowed to play, only watch. Penalties bother hockey players because they would rather play hockey than watch. Keep this hockey comparison in mind when using time-out for your child. Children usually do not like time-out because they would rather play than watch other kids play. So when you use time-out in response to a problem behavior, remove your child from whatever he is doing and have him sit down.

Where should the time-out area be located?

You do not have to use the same location each time. Just make sure the location is convenient for you. For example, using a downstairs chair is inconvenient when the problem behavior occurs upstairs. An adult-sized chair works best, but a step, footstool, bench, or couch will also work. Make sure the area is well-lit and free from all dangerous objects. Also make sure your child cannot watch TV or play with toys.

How long should time-out last?

The **upper** limit should be one **quiet** minute for every year your child has been alive. So if you have a two-year-old, aim for two quiet minutes. Keep in mind, children do not like time-out, and they can be very public with their opinion. So it may take some time to get those two minutes of quiet. This is especially true in the beginning when children do not know the rules and still cannot believe you are doing this to them. For some reason, the calmer you remain, the more upset they are likely to become. This is all part of the process. Discipline works best when you administer it calmly.

So, do not begin the time until your child is calm and quiet. If your child is crying or throwing a tantrum, it does not count toward the required time. If you start the time because your child is quiet but he starts to cry or tantrum, wait until your child is quiet again and then start the time over. Do not let your child leave time-out unless he is calm; your child must remain seated and be quiet to get out of time-out. Some people and programs suggest using timers. Timers can be helpful but are not necessary. If you use one, remember the timer is to remind **parents** that time-out is over, **not children.**

What counts as quiet time?

Generally, quiet time occurs when your child is not angry or upset, and is not yelling or crying. You must decide when your child is calm and quiet. Some children get perfectly still and quiet while in they're in time-out. Other children find it hard to sit still and not talk. Fidgeting and "happy talk" should usually count as being calm and quiet. For example, if your son sings or talks softly to himself, that counts as quiet time. Some children do what we call "dieseling," which is the quiet sniffling that usually follows a tantrum. Since a "dieseling" child is usually trying to stop crying but cannot find the "off" switch, this also should be counted as quiet time.

What if the child leaves the chair before time is up?

Say nothing! Calmly (and physically) return your child to the chair. For children who are two- to four-years old, unscheduled departures from the chair are a chronic problem early in the time-out process. Stay calm and keep returning the child to the chair. If you tire or become angry, invite your spouse (or any adult who is nearby) to assist you as a tag-team partner. If you are alone and become overly tired or angry, retreat with honor. But when help arrives or when your strength returns, set the stage for another time-out.

What if my child misbehaves in the chair?

Say nothing and ignore everything that is not dangerous to child, yourself, and the furniture. I repeat: **Say nothing!** What do I mean by nothing? I mean not anything, the absence of something, the empty set, the amount of money you have when you have spent it all, the result of two minus two or what zero equals. I mean nothing. Most of your child's behavior in the chair is an attempt to get you to react and say something, anything. So expect the unexpected, especially if you are a nagger, screamer, explainer, warner, reasoner, or just a talker. And I mean the unexpected. They may spit up, wet, blow their nose on their clothes (you may be tempted to say "Yecch" but... do not), strip, throw things, make unkind comments about your parenting skills, or simply say they do not love you anymore. Do not worry. They will love you again when their time is up, believe me.

When should I use time-out?

When you first start, use it for only one or two problem behaviors. After your child has learned to "do" time-out, you can expand the list of problem behaviors. In general, problem behaviors fall into three categories: 1) anything dangerous to self or others; 2) defiance and/or noncompliance; and 3) obnoxious or bothersome behavior. Use time-out for "1" and "2" and ignore anything in category "3." If you cannot ignore something, move it into category "2" by issuing a command ("Take the goldfish out of the toilet."). Then if the child does not comply, you can use time-out for noncompliance. Be sure to use time-out as **consistently** as possible. For example, try to place your child in time-out each time a targeted behavior occurs. I realize you cannot be one-hundred percent consistent because it is in our nature to adapt. But be as consistent as you can.

In general, immediately following a problem behavior, tell your child what she did and take her to time-out. (With older children, send them to time-out.) For example, you might say, "No hitting. Go to time-out." Say this calmly and only once. Do not reason or give long explanations to your child. If your child does not go willingly, take her to time-out, using as little force as needed. For example, hold your daughter gently by the hand or wrist and walk to the time-out area. Or, carry her facing away from you (so that she does not confuse a trip to time-out with a hug). As I suggested earlier, avoid giving your child a lot of attention while she is being put in time-out. **Do not** argue with, threaten, or spank your child. And what should you say? Hint: Starts with "No'" and ends with "thing." Answer: **Say nothing!**

What do I do when time is up?

When the time-out period is over, ask your child, "Are you ready to get up?" Your child must answer "Yes" in some way (or nod in agreement) before you give permission to get up. Do not talk about why the child went into time-out, how the child behaved while in time-out, or how you want your child to behave in the future. In other words, do not nag. If your child says "No," answers in an angry tone of voice, or will not answer at all, start time-out over again. If your child chooses to stay in the chair, fine. It is hard to cause real trouble in time-out.

What do I do when my child leaves the chair?

If you placed your child in time-out for not doing what you told him to do, repeat the instruction. This will help teach your child you mean business. It also gives your child a chance to behave in a way that is good for business. If he still does not obey the instruction, then place him in time-out again. When your child obeys your instruction, add in a few other easy-to-follow, one-step commands. If he does them, praise the performance. If not, back to time-out. Generally, use this opportunity to train your child to follow your instructions when those instructions are delivered in a normal tone of voice without being repeated.

The general rule for ending time-out is to **praise** a good behavior. Once time-out is over, reward your children for the kinds of behaviors you want them to use. **Catch them being good.**

Should I explain the rules of time-out to my child?

Before using time-out, you should explain the rules to your child once. At a time when your child is not misbehaving, explain what time-out is (simply), which problem behaviors time-out will be used for, and how long time-out will last. Practice using time-out with your child before using the procedure. While practicing, remind your child you are "pretending" this time. They will still go "ballistic" when you do your first real time-outs, but you will be reassured that you have done your part to explain the fine print.

Summary of Time-out Guidelines

1. Choose time-out areas.
2. Explain time-out (once).
3. Use time-out **every** time the targeted problem behaviors occur.

4. Be specific and brief when you explain why your child must go to time-out.

5. Do not talk to or look at your child during time-out.

6. If your child gets up from the chair, return her to the chair with no talking.

7. Your child must be calm and quiet to leave time-out once time is up.

8. Your child must answer "Yes" politely when you ask, "Would you like to get up?"

9. If you wanted your child to follow an instruction, give him another chance after time-out is over. And, in general, deliver a few other easy-to-follow commands so your child clearly learns who is in charge and who is not.

10. Catch and praise children when they are being good.

Time-out is an effective strategy for teaching toddlers how to calm themselves down because they have to learn to sit alone and calm down before they are free to go. When time-out is implemented correctly, there is no interaction with the child from anyone until the child is calm and quiet. Ultimately, the child learns how to become calm and quiet, valuable skills necessary for life.

One important thing for parents to remember is that completing time-out is a skill or behavior children have to learn how to do. And the only way they can learn how to do time-out is to be put in time-out. As previously stated, it is recommended to practice time-out with children when they are not in trouble. Like most skills, it is easier to exhibit and use a skill when emotions are neutral or positive. It is much more difficult to exhibit a skill when under stress or upset. Children are often upset when they earn time-out, and as a result, they must learn to successfully complete time-out when they are upset. Once they learn how to do this, children will go to time-out readily, sit quietly, and complete time-out within a few minutes or seconds.

Sometimes, parents misinterpret the child's ready cooperation as a sign that time-out is not working. The behavior parents must pay attention to in order to determine whether time out is working is the behavior the child engages in to earn time-out. If the frequency or severity of the problem behavior decreases, time-out is working. If it doesn't decrease or even gets worse, review the time-out guidelines in this chapter to determine where you might be administering time-out incorrectly.

CHAPTER 13

MEDia MattER!

One of the messages I hope you take from this book is that our experiences influence us. The people, situations, and things in the world we are exposed to directly impact what we learn, how we act, what we think, and how we feel. Media are very much a part of all our worlds, especially today and with our youth. The words we read on the printed page (books, newspapers, magazines, billboards) and in the digital world (music lyrics, text messages, emails, Internet) are everywhere – and they matter. Also, the images we see and hear in advertisements, on the Internet, on television, in magazines, and in video games are a significant part of our experience and how we develop.

Once we are exposed to words or images, they are forever a part of us. They influence our thoughts, feelings, and actions. You might recall from an earlier chapter the phrase, "We don't know what we don't know." This is true in so many ways, and media is a powerful source of introducing children and teens to things they didn't know before – both positive and negative.

On the positive side, kids can learn how people have overcome obstacles to fulfill their dreams, stood by their values in the face of all kinds of pressure, and made sacrifices for the benefit or justice of others. The media also can provide lots of negative experiences and influences, like getting what you want by way of cruelty, aggression, and violence; avoiding accountability for poor decisions by lying and deception; and glamorizing alcohol and drug use.

As parents, it is our responsibility to pay attention to our children's exposure to the media and how they are influencing and shaping them. While we can't control everything our children are exposed to at all times, we can influence what they are exposed to in our own homes. This includes what they (and the rest of the family) are allowed to watch on TV; interact with, read, and watch on the Internet; listen to on the radio or iPod; what books, music magazines, and video games they buy; the movies they go to and watch; and other activities they are allowed to participate in outside the home.

Parents can't control all the media their children are or have been exposed to, but you can set limits, be clear with your expectations, and follow through with positive and negative consequences when kids meet or fail to meet those expectations. This is especially important to do with children who have problems with anger and aggression. They need close monitoring and management of what they are exposed to via the media. Let's look at example.

• • •

Anna is a 16- year-old girl who is constantly texting her friends. Often, she can be found texting and messaging her friends on Facebook at the same time. Her friends are kids from school, the neighborhood, and many others she has met online. Even though Anna has never met and doesn't really know the people she met online, Anna readily shares her cell phone number with them. Several of these online friends have asked her for inappropriate pictures and invited her to get together for some "fun." Many nights, Anna is texting late into the night.

When Anna's parents want to check her text messages, she quickly deletes them. When they want to check her Facebook site, she is reluctant to share her password and edits the site before her parents can see it. She certainly won't "friend" her parents on Facebook because then they would see everything on her page.

When Anna isn't texting or on Facebook, she watches lots of TV or listens to her favorite music. She seems to make every effort to stay away from her parents, brother, and sisters. At times, the music that blasts from her bedroom is filled with lyrics that degrade women, promote violence, and glamorize anger and being angry.

Anna also keeps a journal that is full of negative, angry statements about her parents and others. Some of her entries indicate she feels angry all the time and "hates" her parents. Parents of other teens have contacted Anna's parents about cruel texts and messages she has sent their teens via texting or online.

When her parents try to talk with her about cyberbullying, setting limits for cell phone and online use, and being careful about who she shares personal information with, Anna becomes angry and accuses her parents of violating her privacy.

• • •

This example shows how today's media can influence and contribute to a child's anger problem. Here, Anna is being exposed to media that are influencing and reinforcing her anger and aggressive behavior. In turn, she is exposing others to similar messages with her behavior. Is it too late to help kids like Anna? Certainly not. She will likely resist her parents' efforts, but it is important that they help Anna learn how to treat others with respect and use assertive rather than aggressive behavior.

Kids and the Media

Children are always learning. They learn by doing, watching, playing, reading, and listening. We have known for years that what children watch on TV impacts their behavior. Today, the influence of media goes well beyond TV. Children and teens also are exposed to movies, video games, Internet content and gaming, computer games, music and music videos, print media, text images, and others. And the list of new media technologies continues to grow and expand. The challenge for parents is to be aware of all that their children are exposing themselves to, whether that involves what they watch, play, or listen to.

It is impossible in this technological age for anyone to be completely isolated from the media. Television, radio, movies, Internet content, books, magazines, musical formats (CD's, audio files, etc.), newspapers, artwork, and billboards are almost everywhere, bombarding us with messages that inform, entertain, sell a product, or make a statement. Some of the messages carried by the media are positive and educational; others are negative or downright dangerous.

It is up to parents to decide what is right or wrong for their child to see, hear, or read. They know their children best and know what they can handle and understand. Parents are the ones who have to set the boundaries for children's exposure to media and their messages. When children have no guidance, they can be easily influenced by the harmful messages.

While there are many forms of media, the four considered to have the most influence on kids today are television, movies, music, and the Internet.

Television is a fixture in the lives of most children. It can serve as a baby sitter, a teacher, an entertainer, and a shaper of behavior. Unfortunately, the effects it can have are not always positive. As previously mentioned, research indicates that kids who watch a lot of television programs with aggressive and violent content are more likely to use aggressive and violent behaviors with others than kids who aren't exposed to those kinds of programs. And since research shows that kids watch about thirty hours of TV a week, it's a pretty good bet that they'll see some programs with aggressive and violent content.

Even worse may be the way kids become desensitized to aggression and violence. In other words, children become unable to feel compassion or sympathy for people who are hurt or killed in real life because they have seen so many characters get shot, stabbed, blown up, or "killed" on television. In fact, studies on children's viewing habits have found that the average child will witness more than two hundred thousand violent acts and sixteen thousand murders on television before age eighteen.

Violent movies have the same impact. Story lines are built around conflict, and conflict is usually settled with force and graphic violence, the gorier the better. Kids laugh and cheer when the hero blows the villain to pieces with a rocket launcher. They shriek with delight when the killer leaps out of a closet and stabs a screaming teen-age girl. And they rate how "cool" a movie is by its body count and the number of gunshots and explosions. Even movies that are rated PG or PG-13 can contain violent scenes that many parents would find objectionable for younger children.

Music also is very influential, especially among teenagers. Radio stations play songs that are heavy on lyrics about death, suicide, violence (mainly against women), and aggression. Young people can buy CDs or download songs with objectionable material, even though many now carry warning labels. Teens idolize rock stars who promote a lifestyle of violence, drugs, and sex. A number of music videos also have violent themes, and a popular style of music called "gangsta' rap" relies heavily on profanity to describe, and sometimes glorify, violence and gang violence.

Finally, the Internet has opened up a whole new world of experiences – good and bad – for young people. And children can access the Internet with ease any where any time. Cell phones, computers, hand held video games, video gaming systems, and iPods give children and teens ready access to the Internet. The Internet is great for doing research for reports, but kids also can easily access websites that contain violent or pornographic material. And state-of-the-art computer and video games continually push the envelope in terms of mayhem and gore, especially those in which players participate in bloody virtual shootouts with a variety of "enemies."

What can parents do to protect their children from these negative influences? First, they can filter the images and messages that are available to kids. This means knowing the content of and monitoring what kids watch on television, what movies they go to, what kinds of music they listen to, what kinds of books and magazines they read, and what they pull up on the Internet or play on the computer.

So check out the television programs your kids watch and the movies they want to see. Monitoring the television is easiest; it's in your home so you can usually see what your kids are watching, and you can check out the maturity rating for programs ahead of time. Set limits for how much TV your kids can watch. While the average child watches about thirty hours of television a week, that's more than double the maximum of fourteen hours a week experts recommend. For movies, read reviews in the newspaper or magazines, or pull up information about films on the Internet. This can give you a good idea of what the movie is about and whether there is graphic violence or sex or inappropriate language. If possible, view a movie before letting your child see it. Then you can make an informed decision about whether you want your child to see it.

As parents, Dan and I let our children know what TV shows and movies we consider inappropriate for them to watch. For example, content that portrays rude, disrespectful, and angry behavior toward parents and others as acceptable or funny is not allowed. Keep in mind that what goes into your child's mind stays there. That means what your children are exposed to in the way of media becomes part of their learning experience. How it is understood, interpreted, and thought of depends on your child's age and developmental level. However it is taken in, the information stays in and inevitably helps to shape your children's thinking and understanding, and how they interact with their environment.

The more exposure children and teens have to angry and aggressive behavior as popular, effective, and acceptable, the more likely they will be to engage in similar behaviors. Media are powerful portrayers of these kinds of behaviors so make sure you manage how much exposure your children have to them.

Also, listen to some of the music your child likes. Find out something about the artists or groups, especially if you suspect that the lyrics are not appropriate for children and teens. Also, check out song lyrics and find out why certain music carries warning labels. (Lyrics often are printed on inserts that come with a CD, or you can find them on various music websites.) The more information you have, the better decisions you and your child can make about what kind of music you want in your home.

Most homes today have computers that are connected to the Internet, so it's important for you to find out what websites your kids are visiting. Also check out the computer and video games your child might be playing. (And even play them yourself.) Monitor what your child is doing on the computer, even if it's in the bedroom. Awareness is the key here; if you don't know your child is doing something that is potentially harmful, you can't take steps to stop it.

Second, parents should talk to their kids about what they see or hear. For example, if you're watching a TV show or movie together and there's a shooting, ask questions like, "How do think it would feel if a person really got shot?" or "What would really happen if someone shot someone?" or "Is that the way people should treat each other?" This helps kids understand that TV shows and movies are play-acting, and that people actually get hurt or die as a result of real-life aggression and violence.

153

This also is a great opportunity to talk about how people who use violence and aggression in real life face serious consequences, like being arrested and going to jail. For example, children see many television programs and movies where the "hero" seeks revenge. Usually, the plot involves a bad guy who hurts or kills someone who is the good guy's friend, wife, husband, brother, etc. Then the good guy sets out on a mission to even the score. No matter how the good guy gets back at the villain, it is portrayed as being justified and right, and the "hero" rarely faces any negative consequences for his actions. (A study found that the "good guys" initiate about forty percent of the violent acts seen on television, and that consequences of violent behavior are shown only fifteen percent of the time.) Children, especially young kids, must understand that using aggression or violence to get back at someone who has "dissed" or hurt them or someone they like rarely is the right thing to do, and that such behavior can carry a heavy punishment in real life.

Third, do a lot of teaching so your children know what you consider to be appropriate and inappropriate material. As a parent, you can help shape your children's view of the world. If you consistently reinforce the idea that using anger, aggression, and violence are not ways to solve problems, they will be more likely to buy into that idea and make it part of their own belief systems. This makes it easier for children to understand the difference between fantasy violence and reality violence and to make better choices in situations where they become angry or frustrated.

Finally, remember that you control what comes into your house, whether it's through the airwaves or the Internet, or from the video or music store. You can make ultra-violent television shows, movies, music, comic books, computer and video games, and Internet sites off limits because they are inappropriate for children. Discuss your decisions with your kids so they understand your point of view. If your kids are home alone a lot, you can make rules for using the computer, and set limits on how much and what types of television programs they can watch when you're gone. You also can look into blocking objectionable TV programs and Internet sites so that your kids don't have access to them.

As a parent of children who enjoy playing video games, I struggle with the violence my teens are exposed to with these games. Dan or I do take time to watch our kids play so we are informed about the game's content. When Dan and I question the content of the games our teens want to buy or play, they sometimes become annoyed and rationalize their choice by saying things like, "It's not a big deal," "The animation isn't lifelike," or "There's no blood." Still, we all discuss the game, its objective, and who the "good" and "bad" guys are before we make decisions about what to buy or allow our teens to buy. Dan and I don't always agree with our kids but what we decide as parents is what our children must learn to accept.

If your children have a lot of free time, have them ride their bikes, draw, shoot baskets, read, write letters to grandparents, have friends over to play, do chores, or any number of the many activities available to kids. There are so many other things they can do other than being glued to their cell phones, televisions, video games, or computers.

Many children think that watching television or enjoying other forms of entertainment is a God-given right. It's not. For example, there's nothing wrong with having your kids earn their TV time; then television becomes a privilege rather than an electronic baby-sitter that's always blaring in the background.

Media alone won't cause children to express their anger in problematic ways. Parents, friends, siblings, relatives, teachers, peers, and others play a huge role in that, too. That's why setting a good example, establishing clear limits for problem behavior, and teaching your children that managing their anger is their responsibility all go a long way toward helping children learn to effectively and appropriately manage situations when they get angry.

CHAPTER 14

TEaCH PROBLEM SOLVinG

When children have a positive way to solve their problems or figure out how to get what they want, they are less likely to turn to aggression. This chapter discusses a problem-solving method that is easy for parents to teach and easy for kids to learn.

This method is called **SODAS**. The letters stand for **Situation, Options, Disadvantages, Advantages,** and **Solution.** SODAS is a good method because it helps accomplish two goals:

- It gives parents and children a process for solving problems and making decisions together.

- It helps parents teach children how to solve problems and make decisions on their own.

Here is how SODAS works:

Situation

Before you can solve a problem, you must know what the problem is. Ask your child to describe the situation. This step usually takes the longest because kids often use vague or emotional descriptions. You can help by asking open-ended questions like, "What did you do then?" or "What happened next?" Avoid questions that kids can answer with a "Yes" or a "No," or a word that really doesn't mean much like "Fine." The goal here is to define the situation as clearly as possible so the child can come up with the best solution.

It's also a good idea to summarize the information your child provides. Children sometimes become so emotional when talking about a problem that they lose sight of what the actual problem is. Once you've stated the problem in its simplest form, ask the child if your summary is correct.

Options

Oftentimes, kids see a solution as an "all-or-nothing" deal. For example, a child who isn't getting along with a neighbor boy might think that moving out of the neighborhood is the only solution. But every problem usually has several options for solutions. So have your child write down three to four options. Don't make any comments on whether they are good or bad, or whether they will work or not; the purpose here is to get the child to think of ways to solve the problem. If your child has trouble coming up with options, make some suggestions to get him started.

Disadvantages/Advantages

In this step, you help your child look at the pros and cons of each option. This helps the child see the connection between each option and what could happen if that option is chosen.

First, ask your child for her thoughts about each option. (What's good about the option? What's bad? Why would the option work? Why won't the option work?) Then help her list the disadvantages and advantages for each one. Write these down so you both can remember them.

Solution

Now it's time for your child to pick an option to try. Quickly summarize the advantages and disadvantages for each option, and have your child choose the one that he thinks will work best. Make sure your child knows the options and the possible outcomes of each one. If a decision doesn't have to be made right away, let your child take some time to think about his choice. Once the choice is made, you can help him practice using the solution. If the solution involves having your child talk to someone, you can play the part of the other person and respond to what your child says in ways the other person might. This prepares the child for a variety of responses.

After your child tries the solution he picked, check later to see if it worked. This is an excellent time to praise your child for making a decision and following through with it.

A few words of caution: Children sometimes may come up with or want to try options that you don't agree with. In those situations, the general rule is that if the option won't hurt anyone and isn't illegal or contrary to your moral or religious beliefs, then let the child make the choice and learn from his or her decision.

If this process is new to you, begin with a small problem. This gives your child time to feel comfortable with using it. Many kids don't have the patience to think things out. They get angry or frustrated and just want to get it over with. But don't let your kids make quick choices; teach them that it's worth taking some extra time to come up with a solution that is likely to work and doesn't involve angry or aggressive behaviors.

While you will want to encourage your kids to make decisions and solve problems on their own, you need to let them know that you will always be there to help and support them. If a solution does not work out as planned, go back to the SODAS method and find another solution to the problem.

A similar, though slightly abbreviated, version of SODAS is **POP,** which stands for **Problem, Options,** and **Plan.** Again, this decision-making method helps children, especially younger ones, clarify what the problem is, identify the options they have for dealing with it, and then actually following through on their decision with a plan.

SODAS and POP Examples

Let's look at examples of how to use the POP and SODAS problem-solving processes with children who are struggling with issues related to anger.

POP – Brandon

A patient of mine, Brandon (an 8-year-old boy), recently got into trouble at his after-school program for getting mad at and biting a boy two years younger than Brandon. At first glance, you might think the problem is Brandon biting the boy. However, the real problem that needs solving is that the other boy took the ball Brandon was playing with and he wanted it back. Brandon knew what the problem was and he exercised an option: He bit the boy. This resulted in Brandon getting into more trouble.

I used the POP problem-solving method with Brandon to help him better handle similar situations in the future. First, I helped Brandon define the problem **(P)** – the boy took the ball. Next, I asked Brandon to come up with and consider other options **(O)**. These included: let the boy have the ball, ask the boy to give the ball back, ask the teacher for help, tackle the boy, take the ball back by force, and hit the boy. As you can see, many of Brandon options included using force to solve the problem. To help him make a plan **(P),** I encouraged him to think about an option that would help him get the ball back without getting into more trouble. While trying to problem solve with Brandon, he became angry and complained the incident was over and he didn't want to talk about it anymore. He even plugged his ears. Even though I was getting frustrated, I remained calm and said, "Brandon, I can see talking about this is making you mad. We are going to take a break so you can calm down. In a few minutes we will talk about this again."

When Brandon settled down, we tried again. I said, "Brandon, you have done a nice job calming down. We need to make a plan for situations that make you mad." Brandon remained calm and picked an option that wouldn't result in him getting into more trouble: He would nicely ask for the ball back and, if needed, ask the teacher for help. Due to the POP process, Brandon was able to focus on picking an option and plan that worked better and did not lead to more problems and trouble for him and others.

SODAS – Crystal

Crystal, a 15-year-old girl, got angry when her younger sister went into her room without permission and took and wore her new shirt **(situation)**. When Crystal saw her sister in the shirt, Crystal yelled at her sister, grabbed at her, and pulled her hair. Crystal's response was the option she chose in the heat of the moment. Did it work for her? Well, she did express her anger. And it might have even gotten her sister to stay out of her room for a while. But, it didn't stop her sister from borrowing her clothes without permission forever. So, Crystal's parents encouraged her to think of other **options** to solve the problem. These included: fine the sister by having her do Crystal's chores for a day, have the sister give up something of her own, Crystal could take something belonging to her sister, Crystal could break something belonging to her sister, or Crystal could keep the door to her room locked. Next, Crystal and her parents went over the **advantages** and **disadvantages** of all the options. The first three options all would result in negative consequences for the sister and not for Crystal (an advantage). However, the disadvantage of these three options is that Crystal's sister will likely continue to take Crystal's belongings and risk the chances of getting caught. The next two options would result in Crystal getting into trouble, and her sister will likely continue to take Crystal's belongings (both disadvantages). The only potential advantage to these two options is Crystal might feel better in the moment. The final option would work to keep Crystal's sister out of Crystal's belongings (an advantage); however, locking the door would be inconvenient and Crystal would have to make sure her belongings were always in her room (both disadvantages). Ultimately, Crystal decided (and her parents agreed) the best **solution** was to have her sister do Crystal's chores each time she takes something without permission.

When you sit down and use a problem-solving method like SODAS or POP with children, you do more than just strengthen their ability to make better judgments. You strengthen your relationship with them as well. You want children to share with you so that you know what's going on in their lives. The parent who is available and involved is much more likely to calm an angry child and teach him or her to deal with problems assertively.

CHAPTER 15

KNOW WHERE YOUR CHILDREN ARE

We've already discussed the importance of monitoring the TV programs and movies your kids watch, the music they listen to, the books they read, the video games they play, and the Internet sites they visit. Now let's talk about a different kind of monitoring, one that involves keeping track of your kids' behaviors, who they hang around with, what's happening at school, what they do with their free time, and how they see the world around them.

Whether your kids are younger or older, monitoring their activities lets them know that you care about them and their safety. In fact, it's a good idea to remind your children from time to time that you want to know what they're involved in because you love them. If kids don't understand your reasons, they might think that all you're doing is spying on them, a situation that can cause mistrust and bad feelings.

As I said earlier, you are the biggest influence in your child's life. If you don't know what your kids are doing and aren't involved in their lives (aside from making sure they have a roof over their heads and food on the table), someone else may take over that role. When that someone is another youth (or a group of youths) who are up to no good, trouble is likely to be just around the corner.

Checking on your kids is a great way to help them avoid negative peer pressure. When you know what's going on, you can help your children head off problems before they occur by teaching them how to make good decisions when someone tries to talk them into doing something harmful or destructive. Kids can become very confused when they're being pulled in different directions by parents and teachers on one side and their friends and peers on the other. They often will need to sort through a confusing mix of conflicting thoughts and feelings. Informed parents are better able to help their kids make good decisions.

Monitoring also provides you with more opportunities to catch your kids being good and to reward them for good behavior. This reinforces positive behaviors and makes it more likely that your kids will use them in the future.

Obviously, talking with your children at meals, bedtime, or when you're just sitting around is the best way to keep up with what's going on in their lives. But you can't be with your kids every minute, especially when they go out. You need to know what they're doing outside of the home. So get to know your child's friends and their parents, and set and enforce rules and curfews for going out.

One parent who had four teenagers came up with a great way to take care of these situations. She posted a note on the refrigerator (a spot she knew the kids would visit often). The note read: "Before you ask me to go anywhere, be prepared to tell me where you are going, how you'll get there and back, when you'll be home, what you'll be doing, and who you'll be with." This parent had a pretty good idea of what her teens were doing when they weren't at home.

Parents also can make a point of talking with their kids when they get home about what happened while they were gone. This should be a conversation, not a confrontation or an interrogation. Children have to know that you trust them, and even when they make mistakes (and they will), they have to know that you love them.

CHAPTER 16

THE ROLE OF SPIRITUALITY

This chapter is a brief introduction to the important role that spirituality can play in the lives of families. It is written from the Christian perspective as I was raised Catholic and Dan and I chose to raise our children in the Catholic faith. If you are of another faith, please keep reading and interpret or apply the content to your own spiritual life.

I believe spirituality is a central component of healthy functioning, much like people think about medical, physical, and mental health. You will likely notice that the content in this chapter is discussed and presented in a similar fashion to the content in the rest of the book, where the focus is on teaching children by word and example. This is just as important with spirituality as it is with any other facet of parenting.

If you do not endorse spirituality or a faith life, keep reading anyway. You might discover something you hadn't considered before. If the chapter content leads you to wanting to learn more, I suggest you start by talking with friends or relatives you trust who have an active faith life. Or, you might try attending a local church or faith center and talking with a minister or religious leader there to learn more.

Attending church, saying prayers, and learning about faith have always been a part of my life. My parents modeled engagement in these activities and taught us to value an active faith life. We prayed together as a family, attended church weekly, and participated in religion classes. Both my parents were involved in our parish by singing in the choir, teaching religion classes, coordinating the religion program, taking care of the church, and participating in religious and faith development activities.

At home, references to right and wrong often went back to explaining what constituted a sin. As children, we were encouraged to pray for help, guidance, strength, courage, and forgiveness when we were struggling, lost something, were fearful or sick, or were in need in some other way.

As the years have gone by, I value my faith more and more. Dan and I have made faith something we value as a couple and as parents. We have tried to raise our children to value faith as well, through our actions, teaching, and an open trust in God's will for our lives.

Why Bother with Spirituality?

Spiritual beliefs help guide the development of values and morals, which include treating others with respect, meaning not using verbal or physical aggression with others; responding with forgiveness rather than anger and revenge when offended by others; and respecting life, including human life and all other species and forms of life. These kinds of morals and values need to be taught to kids. For example, most younger children don't know how to be gentle, careful, and loving with small animals like kittens, puppies, and bunnies. This actually involves skills children need to learn. They don't understand their grip strength or how to properly hold small animals gently and safely, and they need to be given the opportunity to handle animals with adult supervision in order to learn how. When adults teach these skills well, children learn that those smaller and more vulnerable than them require care and protection and are not to be targets for aggression or bullying. This kind of teaching is part of the larger message parents should send to their children: That anger and aggression are unacceptable ways to deal with other people, handle situations, and solve problems.

Spirituality also gives people a source of accountability and community. Many religions have regular services where members come together to honor their common beliefs and traditions. However, living an active spiritual life means more than just attending services. It also means being aware of your thoughts, words, and actions toward others and working to treat them with respect and love. This can also be called demonstrating "integrity" – or being and doing who and what you say you are.

Finally, striking out against others in anger or frustration is in conflict with most spiritual beliefs and their teachings. This basic tenet goes a long way toward helping children and teens, especially those who struggle with anger and aggression problems, grow and develop into caring, loving, and respectful individuals.

Faith and Anger

So, how does faith fit with helping angry children? I believe there are a number of connections and will discuss four of them here. First, I believe that all children are gifts from God. It can be challenging for parents to remember this at times, especially when your child is angry and aggressive and says hurtful things. Reminding yourself that your child is a gift to you and the world and is a person to be loved, may help you manage your own emotions more effectively, especially during stressful times.

Even when your child engages in problem behavior, that child is still a gift. What your child hasn't learned yet is how to behave more acceptably in certain situations. Oftentimes, we are quick to decide that there is something wrong with our child rather than her behavior as illustrative of what she has and has not yet learned. When we think about kids and their behavior from the standpoint of **learning** rather than personal traits, we have the opportunity to impact our child in a much more positive, healthy, and effective manner.

Second, faith can help parents by giving them the belief that God does not give them more than they can handle. That means if you have a difficult or angry child, you can handle it. There is comfort and acceptance in this belief. You might find the content of this book or others sufficient to help you teach your child how to manage anger more effectively. Or, you might discover you need additional help or resources and have to seek out other services. Your faith can help you feel reassured and confident that you are fully capable of doing your part in helping your child.

Third, forgiveness is a central part of spirituality and an active faith life. Parents have tons of opportunities to forgive their children because they will make mistakes on their journey to becoming adults. It's important for children to observe their parents modeling forgiveness. When you forgive, you model how your child should do it, too. Also, when you offer forgiveness through your words or actions to someone who might have offended you, you are again modeling forgiveness for your child. Through modeling and direct teaching, you can help your children learn how to forgive someone who has offended them. Ultimately, your faith in forgiveness teaches kids that forgiveness and letting go of hurt, frustration, resentment, and anger help them move forward in a more peaceful, loving, and caring manner.

Finally, spirituality is an important dimension of being human. Belief in a "higher power" matters. A belief that there is good and evil and right and wrong helps to guide our values and moral development as individuals and as a society. As with other skills and knowledge children acquire, spirituality also has to be taught for them to learn how it can help and what to do to get those benefits. The earlier you do this with children, the better. Letting kids decide about their spiritual life when they get older without providing information or a foundation from you can set them up for making uniformed decisions. You wouldn't wait to let children decide as adults whether or not they want to go to school. How could your children appreciate the value of all they can learn from education if they never have any exposure to it?

Exposure, participation, and teaching are also important for children to understand the value and benefits of spirituality. There is no guarantee that all children will choose to continue practicing a specific spirituality or faith – or any at all – when they become adults. But, it does allow kids to better understand what it is they are accepting or rejecting.

What You Can Do

What can parents do to create an atmosphere that will enable children and families to grow in faith and morality? Here are a few suggestions:

- **Let your children see the importance of faith in your life.** As you live out your faith, your children will likely see you pray, pray with you, and attend services with you. Being of service to others and living in accord with your faith beliefs are also visible ways of modeling the importance of spirituality for your children.

- **Teach your children to pray.** When you think of prayer, you might first think of ritual prayers like those said at bedtime, before meals, and during religious services or ceremonies. Prayer also can be much less formal. Prayer is about building a personal relationship with God. So,

171

talking to God as much as possible and at any time is a good way to build this relationship. Thanking God when you are happy, asking for help when you are sad, angry, or frustrated, are equally good times to build your relationship. Prayer can take the form of reading the Bible or other books on spirituality, meditating, and singing. Prayer is a means of praising, offering thanks, expressing gratitude, and making requests or petitions.

- **Be active in your religion with your children.** Religious services and classes provide opportunities for children to learn about the foundations of their faith, how to practice their faith, and how to continue to grow in the understanding and expression of their faith. Many religions offer and support a variety of education, service, spiritual, and social activities that help promote a sense of community and meet the spiritual needs of their members (of all ages). Being involved as a participant as well as a volunteer provides opportunities for learning and spiritual growth for you and your children.

- **Live and teach your children the Ten Commandments.** God gave us ten clear commandments to follow. When we live according to these commandments, we are loving God, our families, and our neighbors as God has called us to do. In the context of anger, it is difficult to express anger at others and follow the Ten Commandments at the same time.

- **Teach your child to practice random acts of kindness.** In general, people tend to notice and remember the things that go wrong more than they do the things that go well. However, random acts of kindness – or doing simple, positive things for others for no reason other than to be polite or kind – tend to get noticed by people on the receiving end. These people are then more likely to do something kind for someone else – or "pay it forward." Modeling random acts of kindness is a great way for you to teach your children the importance of doing the same. Some simple acts might include letting someone who is in rush step in front of you in line, holding the door for someone as you enter a building, or simply offering a smile to a stranger. It doesn't take much to spread a little kindness. And you know the power that such acts can have on people. Just think of a time someone did something kind for you. Chances are it made you feel better and you were more likely to do something kind for someone else. This is an important lesson you can pass on to your kids.

Spiritual growth is an essential part of every child's life, as important as physical, emotional, social, and academic growth. Spiritual development adds meaning to the other areas of a person's life. Parents give their children a great gift when they teach them how to grow and develop as spiritual beings with a sense of God-given purpose.

In our society, being strong in faith is not always popular; it would be nice if it were. As parents, we can teach our children to value their spirituality and a faith-filled life through our words and actions. Helping children build healthy, moral lives is good for them as individuals and for society as a whole.

SECTION III

TEACH SO YOUR CHILDREN WILL LEARN

CHAPTER 17

Take a Teaching Approach

When it comes right down to it, one of the biggest parts of parenting is teaching. When parents think about teaching, they often think it is only about correcting a child's problem behavior. While correcting misbehavior is an important part of teaching, you are also teaching when you praise good behavior. For example, if you don't pay attention when children play cooperatively, you are teaching them that behavior is not important to you. However, if you notice and praise them when they play nicely together, you are teaching them how important such behavior is to you. When you deal with frustration or disappointment – either calmly and optimistically or with angry outbursts – you are also teaching these behaviors to your children.

Parents can also teach by specifically instructing children how to use social skills that will improve or replace their angry behavior. This chapter focuses on the kind of teaching that's done in a specific, direct manner. Teaching to problem behaviors is difficult enough, but the task becomes even harder when a parent is trying to prevent or deal with angry and aggressive behaviors. Parents need a plan of action and practical, effective strategies.

In this chapter, we will discuss what you can and should do when your child becomes angry and engages in problem behavior. Keep in mind, however, that this chapter does not stand alone. Everything we've discussed so far in this book needs to be put into place, too, for you to best deal with kids who are angry or acting out in an aggressive manner, verbally or physically, toward you, others, animals, or property. So, in addition to this chapter's information, you are encouraged to draw on the content of the other chapters.

A Teaching Approach

Not all parents know how to appropriately respond to their child's anger and problem behavior with teaching that's consistent and effective. In fact, when parents try to correct children, many do something different each time or they end up yelling and arguing with children. Sometimes, this might work to stop the problem behavior temporarily, but it doesn't teach why the angry behavior is inappropriate and what children should do instead. When children fail to learn and develop necessary life skills, parents become frustrated, and family relationships suffer.

Concerned parents want constructive, appropriate ways to respond when their children get angry or aggressive and misbehave. That's why using a teaching approach works so well for you and your children. Correcting problem behavior though teaching works best in situations where children are doing something they shouldn't do or are not doing something they should do. A few of those specific situations include:

- Not following instructions.
- Doing something that could harm someone or themselves.
- Refusing to accept criticism.
- Arguing with your decisions.
- Refusing to accept responsibility for their behavior.

- Lying.
- Not letting you know where they are.

As you can see, a number of these relate directly to some of the angry and aggressive behavior we've been talking about. A teaching approach gives parents a structured, flexible plan for dealing with anger and aggression and many other kinds of inappropriate behaviors. Used consistently (meaning whenever problem behavior occurs), a teaching approach can help reduce anger and aggression and enable children to learn positive ways to get what they want or to settle differences with others.

Let's discuss a plan of action and some strategies you can use as part of your teaching approach. First, it's important for you to remain calm when anger and problem behavior occurs. Remember, your child's behavior is about skills (or lack of) and learning history – it is not about you. Self-talk is an excellent calming strategy you can use during difficult situations. For example, you might say to yourself, "This is not about me. My son is angry and has not yet learned how to manage and express his anger appropriately. My job is to teach him how to do this by my own actions and how I handle the situation." Using self-talk like this can help you stay composed and focused on teaching skills.

Also, when your child throws a tantrum or your teen starts yelling, just listen quietly. This can help you avoid doing or saying something that might add fuel to your child's anger. Keep in mind that your child will want you to react in some way other than with calm and silence, and that this kind of response might frustrate him or her. Even so, it's still the best response because it allows your child to learn more readily personal responsibility for behavior and emotions. It is difficult for children to blame you for their angry outbursts or temper tantrums when you contributed only a calm, quiet presence.

Another strategy to employ is to calmly give simple instructions that direct your child to do the opposite of any problematic behavior. For example, if your daughter is yelling, you can calmly say, "You are yelling, lower your voice." Or, "Please soften your expression."

If this doesn't work, try taking a break from the interaction. This often helps to de-escalate emotions and calm the situation. With younger children, you might need to send them to their room or a particular place to sit for a time-out until you determine they are calm. For teens, you might say something like, "I want to be able to talk to you about this calmly, so I am going to take a break. I'll check in with you in fifteen minutes."

You may be tempted to tell your child, "You need to calm down." If this instruction worked, you probably wouldn't be reading this book. So, instead of saying that, simply deliver consequences to teach your child to settle down. With younger children, it is recommended to institute time-out for any yelling, hitting, or other behavior you have determined is unacceptable. Do not give warnings for serious problem behavior that breaks a rule in your house, just deliver the time-out consequence. For very young children, you might say, "No hitting, time-out," and nothing more. For school-age children, you might give a consequence that limits access to a privilege and/or requires additional chores to be completed. Here, you might say something like, "Yelling and throwing things are not appropriate. You have earned an extra chore."

Earlier, I suggested that if your child becomes violent or physically aggressive, you should call the police. With a young or small child, I don't think that is necessary or appropriate. Instead, call the police only when you think your child is capable of inflicting serious injury to self or others. This helps to ensure that everyone is safe and no one gets hurt.

It is important to "ride out the storm." And you can do this by remaining composed, providing simple "to do" commands and instructions, and delivering consequences your child earns in a calm, confident manner. All this helps you handle difficult situations in effective ways that allow the learning process to work best.

It's important to remember that it will take time for your child to calm down once he or she has become angry. When a person's nervous system engages in the "flight or fight" response, it takes time to reverse the process and settle back down. That's why it is a good idea to allow your child to take a break, use deep breathing, take a walk, listen to music, or engage in some other activity that will help the cooling down process.

Also, you should decide ahead of time what calming strategies you are willing to let your child use to calm down, whether that's taking a walk around the block, going to the bedroom to listen to music, writing in a journal, or drawing. That way, when your child is angry, you can give a reminder on what she agreed earlier to do to cool down. Once your child uses the calming strategy and settles down, deliver a positive consequence to reinforce its use.

A few more words about consequences: We have been talking about delivering negative consequences for angry and aggressive behavior and giving positive consequences for using calming strategies. Remember, children and teens don't become angry for no reason – something happens first. Perhaps they earned a negative consequence for being late or were reprimanded for taking something without asking permission. When the dust settles, it's very important you remember to enforce the consequence your child earned for the problem behavior that triggered the angry response. If you don't, children will learn that getting angry gets them off the hook for whatever they originally did wrong.

The Teaching Approach in Action

Let's take a look at two examples, one for a younger child and the other for a teen, to see what the teaching approach just discussed might look and sound like.

Seven-year-old Jimmy pushes eight-year-old Latonda because she has a ball he wants.

- **The first step is to have Jimmy stop pushing Latonda.**
You must have Jimmy's full attention before you continue
teaching, and you always want to stop any behavior that
could hurt someone. An effective way to get Jimmy to
stop is to give him a specific instruction that interrupts his
pushing; for example, "Jimmy, come here." Or "Jimmy
keep your hands to yourself."

- **When you have Jimmy's attention,** and he is no longer
pushing and is responding to your instructions, **let him
know pushing is not okay and deliver a consequence.**
In this case, you would use time-out as a consequence.
It's very important to specifically describe to Jimmy the
problem behavior so he clearly understands why he is in
trouble. Telling him he is being "naughty" is too vague.
Telling him "pushing is not okay" is much more specific.

  As you might recall, consequences are the result of
a person's behavior. They can occur naturally (a skinned
knee resulting from falling down on the sidewalk) or
they can be purposely given (a time-out). In the teaching approach, consequences are purposely given to show
children there is a connection between what they do and
what happens to them or others. Here, you could have
Jimmy go to time-out for several minutes until he is completely calm.

- **Once Jimmy has completed his time-out and is completely calm, describe to him what he should do the
next time he wants something someone else has.** This
gives him a choice so he doesn't have to respond only
with negative behavior(s). You could tell Jimmy, "Next
time, you can politely ask for the ball or wait until
Latonda is done playing with it."

- **Give a reason for using the new behavior.** This is where a child learns about the benefits of using the new behavior. For a younger child like Jimmy, the reasons that mean the most will be those that spell out what good things will happen to him. This is called a "self-centered" reason. In this example, a good reason for having Jimmy ask for the ball politely is that Latonda is more likely to give him the ball. When parents have used the teaching approach for a while, they should begin giving "other-centered" reasons. These reasons explain how others will benefit when a youth uses an appropriate behavior. Teaching other-centered reasons helps children understand that their behavior can have a positive effect on others, and that it is good to do something for another person. (More on the importance of giving reasons later.)

- **Practice the new behavior with Jimmy.** Practice helps children learn the new behavior and increases the likelihood they will remember to use it next time. You could tell Jimmy to pretend that you are Latonda and have the ball he wants. Then have Jimmy politely ask you for the ball, the same way he would if he was actually talking to Latonda. If Jimmy forgets what to say or do, start over and have him try it again. If he does a good job, praise him for practicing.

This was a simple example of how to use the teaching approach and its strategies. The consequences and instructions you give might be somewhat different with an older child or a child who is accustomed to your teaching, but the basic structure and approach are the same. Your ability as a parent to use the teaching approach naturally and consistently will determine how much success you have with it.

Here's another example, this time with an older youth. We've included the strategies again to demonstrate what the dialogue might sound like.

Mom overhears her fifteen-year-old son, Brandon, angrily threaten to beat up his younger brother if the boy doesn't give him some money. Mom approaches Brandon and lets him know she wants to talk with him.

Stop and/or describe the problem behavior.

MOM: "Brandon, just now I heard you telling Bobby that you were going to beat him up if he didn't give you some money. We need to talk about this."

BRANDON: "Yeah, but I didn't mean it."

Give a consequence.

MOM: "Thanks for being honest about what you said, and I am glad you didn't mean it. However, that kind of behavior is not allowed in our family. For threatening your brother, you have earned two extra chores and are grounded for two days. That means not having anyone over and not going anywhere, except for school. I also want you to apologize to Bobby. Do you understand?"

BRANDON: "Yeah."

Describe the behavior the child should use.

MOM: "What did you need the money for?"

BRANDON: "John has a new CD. I heard it at his house yesterday and wanted to buy it. I don't have any money but I knew Bobby did."

MOM: "Brandon, you know that there are a lot of things you can do around the house to earn money for a CD. The next time you need some money, you should ask me or Dad what chores need to be done and do them."

BRANDON: "Okay."

Give a reason for using the appropriate behavior.

MOM: "Working around the house is an honest way to earn some money. And it's wrong to threaten others like that; it just scares your brother and makes him afraid of you. Do you understand?"

BRANDON: "Yes."

Practice the new behavior.

MOM: "Let's pretend you need some money to go to a movie with your friends. What would you do and what would you say?"

BRANDON: "I'd come to you or Dad and say, 'Some of the guys are going to a movie but I don't have any money. What can I do around the house to earn some?'"

MOM: "Nice job! Now please go and apologize to your brother."

In this example, Brandon paid attention, cooperated, and accepted his consequences without arguing. But teaching doesn't always go this smoothly. Sometimes, your child won't want to listen to you. He may get even more angry or upset. When this happens, you will have to decide whether it is better to continue your teaching to the problem behavior or adjust your teaching to first show your child how to calm down and regain self-control. We will discuss how and when to do that in the next chapter.

Helpful Hints

As we discussed at the beginning of the chapter, your own behaviors while teaching to your child will have a major impact on whether he or she pays attention and learns what you are trying to teach. Here are some hints for how to make your teaching compassionate, meaningful, and effective.

Be flexible.

As your children change, so will your teaching. Continue to use the teaching approach but feel free to experiment. For instance, if you find that your son responds better and stays calmer when you deliver consequences at the end of an interaction when he has had time to cool down rather than when he is still angry, go with it. No one knows your child better than you. Adjust your teaching in the ways that best meet what you and your child need.

Remember to give reasons.

Giving reasons helps kids understand why they should learn and use positive behaviors. Reasons by themselves don't change behavior, but they can have a big impact when parents use them in their teaching. Kids want to know why they should behave a certain way; they like it when someone gives them a good reason for doing something, and they are more likely to accept reasons that are fair and make sense.

There are two types of reasons: self-centered and other-centered. Reasons that are **self-centered** point out a personal benefit for the youth. For example, a parent might tell his daughter that if she follows an instruction to clean her room right away, she'll have more time to do something she wants to do. This reason is personal and gives the youth an incentive to follow through with the desired behavior.

Self-centered reasons usually work best when parents are just starting to use a teaching approach. (The child's age, developmental ability, and personal needs are other factors to consider.) When kids regularly hear reasons for why they should behave a certain way, it helps them better understand the relationship between what they do and what happens to them. As children begin to experience the benefits of using new behaviors, parents can begin to use more other-centered reasons.

Other-centered reasons point out how a youth's behavior may affect others, either positively or negatively. For example, a parent might say: "If you talk softly instead of yelling, you won't bother your sister when she's trying to do her homework" or "If you steal from a store, you hurt the people who own it. Selling the items is the way they make money to buy food for their families."

Sometimes, it's a good idea to pair other-centered reasons with self-centered reasons. Here's an example: "If you share your toys with your friends when they come over, they'll have more fun playing with you (other-centered) and they'll want to play with you more often (self-centered)."

Studies have shown that children whose parents use other-centered reasons are more likely to show more mature moral development and less aggression. As children engage in positive behaviors and experience the positive consequences of doing so, engaging in the behavior itself makes the child feel good. We have no way of knowing how many times a child will need to engage in the positive behavior and experience the positive consequences before using the behavior makes the child feel good. But we do know that over time this outcome does occur. Helping the child realize other benefits of using behavior for herself and others helps the process move along quicker. Along the way, children develop a conscience and a value system that helps them learn right from wrong and how to make healthy choices. The child begins to act out of concern for others because it makes her feel good and because it is the right thing to do. Eventually, kids treat other people better because they want to, not just because they will earn something positive or avoid a negative consequence.

Teach, don't preach.

Kids don't like long speeches, especially ones that start with, "When I was your age...." It's best to keep your teaching brief and to the point. A lot of kids, especially younger ones, don't have a long attention span, so it's a good idea to stay on point and complete your teaching. Teaching may take longer if you are dealing with a serious behavior, but that's where flexibility comes in. Always be prepared for the unexpected.

Stick to one issue.

Believe it or not, kids sometimes don't want to listen to their parents' teaching. They may say things like, "You don't love me," or "My friends' parents are a lot nicer than you" to get you sidetracked off the topic. But stick with what you want to teach. If your child really wants to discuss other issues, tell him you will sit down later and talk about them.

Provide a chance for the child to earn back part of a consequence.

If your child pays attention, works hard to learn a new behavior, and does well during practice, you can reduce the consequence. For instance, in our earlier example, Brandon earned two extra chores and was grounded for two days for threatening his brother. If Brandon did a good job of listening and practicing, and then sincerely apologized to his brother, his mom could reduce the consequence to one extra chore and one day of grounding. (A good rule of thumb is to reduce up to half of the original consequence.) This is a good way to teach children to make up for their mistakes or problem behaviors, and provides an added incentive to participate and learn new behaviors.

Be consistent.

Once you start using a teaching approach for problem behavior, it is important to use it whenever a problem behavior occurs. Teaching to some problem behaviors and letting others go will confuse kids and undermine what you are trying to accomplish. When you are consistent, kids begin to understand what you expect of them. This improves their cooperation and makes teaching more pleasant and effective in the long run.

Praise improvements in behavior.

When you are correcting problem behavior with a child who easily or often becomes angry, work to praise the child's calm voice tone or attention to you early in the interaction before intense anger flares up. If the child appropriately asks to separate from you to cool down and use a calming strategy, praise her. Or, when you direct the child to repeat a statement in a calm tone of voice and she does so, praise her compliance and any improvement in voice tone or volume, even if you instruct her to try again. Always be on the lookout for opportunities to praise your children when they use or attempt to use positive behaviors.

Use consequences and follow through.

It may be difficult sometimes to deliver consequences to your child for problem behavior. You may even feel guilty about it. But remember that children must learn that there is a connection between what they do and what happens to them. This will be true all of their lives. Consequences help children make that connection and understand that their behavior affects them and others.

As noted earlier, negative consequences usually involve taking away a privilege or adding an extra chore. Taking away a privilege could mean grounding, having your child go to time-out, or losing TV or computer time. Extra chores could include vacuuming, cleaning the bathroom, washing the car, helping a brother or sister with a chore, mowing the lawn, or cleaning the garage.

Don't be afraid to deliver consequences and follow through with them. Your kids will not like earning consequences, especially if you haven't delivered them in the past. But consistently teaching and using consequences will eventually bring about the positive changes you want to see in your kids' anger and behavior.

The teaching approach and strategies offered here are not miracle "cures" for anger, aggression, and problem behavior. They are only tools that give parents something to work with as they try to prevent or reduce angry, aggressive and other problem behaviors in children. Becoming a better teacher will help you become a better parent. But teaching must be done with sincerity and love. Children know when you're just going through the motions; they have to know that you are genuinely concerned about them for the teaching you do to work. Remember that teaching does not occur in a vacuum; it happens within the relationship you have with your kids. The stronger that relationship is, the more effective your teaching will be.

CHAPTER 18

WHEN CHILDREN LOSE CONTROL

Dad asks Maria, twelve-years old, to take some clothes out of the dryer and fold them. Maria, who is watching TV, ignores him. In a little louder voice, Dad again asks Maria to help. Maria yells, "Can't you see I'm watching my show? I always have to do all the d--- chores!" Dad sighs and walks away, and Maria goes back to her TV program.

• • •

Mom tells sixteen-year-old Jason that he has to hurry or he'll be late for school. Jason responds, "Would you get off my back? The h--- with school. I don't care if I'm late." This makes Mom mad and she yells, "Don't you dare talk to me that way. Get moving right now!" Jason raises his fist and screams, "Leave me alone! You can't tell me what to do!" Mom threatens to ground Jason for two weeks if he doesn't "shut his big mouth." Now Jason steps toward his mom and shouts, "You better back off right now and get the h--- away from me!" Mom gives up and retreats to the kitchen.

• • •

Eight-year-old Samuel is watching television when his older brother, Carlos, walks up and grabs the remote control from him. Samuel yells and jumps up, and Carlos punches him in the shoulder several times. Mom hears all this from the kitchen and stomps into the living room. By this time, both boys are hitting each other and wrestling on the floor. Mom begins screaming that she's had it with their fighting over the TV. When the boys ignore her and continue to fight, she separates them, slaps each on the arm, and goes back to the kitchen. Carlos, who still has the remote control, plops onto the couch, sticks his tongue out at Samuel, and changes the channel.

● ● ●

Just before dinner, four-year-old Beth asks if she can have a cookie. Her father says, "No. We will be eating dinner soon." Beth stomps her feet and yells, "I'm hungry now! I want a cookie now!" She proceeds to climb up on the counter and grab a cookie from the cookie jar. Her father approaches her to take the cookie away and Beth slaps at him while quickly shoving the cookie in her mouth. Beth's father says, "I said 'No.' Hitting is not nice." He takes Beth off the counter and away from the cookie jar, then walks away.

● ● ●

These are all examples of what can happen when a parent has had little success in stopping angry and aggressive behavior. In the first example, Dad decided to escape as soon as Maria shouted at him. To him, her yelling was a "punishing" act, and it was easier and less painful for him to get away from it rather than to confront it. In the second example, Mom and Jason took turns trying to top each other with negative behaviors until one of them finally backed down. Jason won the battle when he threatened his mom. In the third example, Mom lashed out at Samuel and Carlos, first yelling at them about arguing and fighting, then slapping the boys. She may have stopped the fight, but she didn't give any consequences or teach the boys a positive way to settle their differences. And Carlos, who started the argument, was rewarded for his angry and aggressive behavior because he got to keep the remote control he took from his brother. In the final example, Beth is told "No" but takes what she wants, and her father is unsuccessful in preventing her problem behavior. Ultimately, she gets what she wants and her father's attempt to teach positive behavior has very little impact.

If these are the wrong ways to respond to serious problem behaviors, what is the right way? You could try teaching and correcting the problem behaviors as we've discussed in previous chapters. And in some situations, this teaching might work. But if a child is angry and uncooperative, and beyond the point of following instructions or paying attention to what you're saying, you might not get very far. This is especially true with an angry child. Usually, when behaviors like yelling, swearing, hitting, throwing things, or stubbornly refusing to follow instructions continue as you try to teach, it signals that you do not have instructional control and the child is far too emotional to benefit from teaching. When children (and adults) are this upset, one way to think about it is that they have lost self-control. When this happens, you must go a step beyond correcting problem behaviors. A teaching method developed by Boys Town that I recommend to parents is **Teaching Self-Control.**

Teaching Self-Control

Teaching Self-Control can help parents accomplish two goals. First, it provides you with an approach that gives the child time to calm down and defuse what is often a very emotional situation. I have stated in previous chapters that children are always learning. Even when they are angry, they are still learning from what you do and say. When children are upset, they are not receptive to the verbal teaching described in the previous chapter. By following the approach described in the Teaching Self-Control approach, you are modeling staying calm, taking time to calm down, following through in addressing the problem behavior, and specifically teaching alternative ways to manage the situation.

The examples at the beginning of this chapter reveal what each of the children learned as they used anger to get what they wanted or to avoid tasks they didn't want to do. Teaching Self-Control allows children and parents time to retreat, settle down, and come back together in a more positive and less emotional frame of mind.

The second goal of Teaching Self-Control is to help children learn what they can do when they get angry or upset to help themselves calm down on their own. Parents and other responsible adults are not always going to be around when children find themselves in situations where things aren't going well. Teaching Self-Control also shows children that angry behavior leads to negative consequences and doesn't lead to getting what they want. Over time, Teaching Self-Control helps kids learn how to identify and express their feelings in an assertive manner instead – skills that are necessary for success at home, in school, on the playground, and in the workplace. Whether you are trying to prevent aggression or correct angry and aggressive behaviors, Teaching Self-Control gives you a structured plan for responding when your child refuses to listen to you and follow instructions, or "blows up" and completely loses self-control.

The Steps to Teaching Self-Control

There are two key parts to Teaching Self-Control: taking time to allow your child to calm down and follow-up teaching. We'll talk about each part in detail later. First, let's take a brief look at what often happens when a child gets angry and yells at the parent or refuses to do what was asked.

In these situations, a child is certainly not interested in, and in some cases, not capable of discussing the situation rationally. A great deal of talking by the parent does little to improve the situation. Often, the more the parent talks, the louder the child yells and the angrier she becomes. The more the child yells, the louder the parent talks – until the parent is yelling, too. This unpleasant exchange of words and actions continues to intensify until someone gives up, gives in, or storms off. It can be the parent who walks out of the room in disgust and anger. Or, it can be the child who angrily stomps off to the bedroom and slams the door shut. In cither case, the problem has gotten worse, not better. If you've had to deal with a child who will not cooperate, you know how helpless it feels at these emotionally intense times.

Teaching Self-Control gives parents a way to stop the yelling or arguing, hopefully before the problem gets worse. Please keep in mind, this approach can be used at any time, the earlier the better. It also provides parents with a structured method for helping their children and teens identify how they're feeling and behaving as wells as how to express their emotions in ways that are helpful, not hurtful.

When to Use Teaching Self-Control

Teaching Self-Control should be used when children refuse to cooperate with you, either passively or aggressively. In passive situations, they simply ignore you. In aggressive situations, they actively refuse to listen and may use yelling, threatening, hitting, and other angry and aggressive behaviors to get what they want.

Teaching Self-Control is appropriate in these two types of situations:

1. When a child exhibits problem behavior and will not respond to your corrective teaching; instead, the child continues to get angry or the problem behavior gets worse.

2. When a child "blows up" – has a sudden and intense emotional outburst – and refuses to do anything that the parent asks.

Think about times when your children got upset when you corrected their behavior or asked them to do something. What triggered their negative or angry behavior? What exactly did they do? How did you respond? Looking back at past blow-ups can help you plan for and practice how you will deal with them in the future. Ways to help prevent blow-ups include teaching proactively (see Chapter 11) to help your child learn more appropriate ways to respond when feeling angry or upset, and remaining calm yourself. However, once your child does have an emotional outburst, it's time to use the steps of Teaching Self-Control.

The Steps of Teaching Self-Control

Teaching Self-Control has two goals and two parts. The goals of Teaching Self-Control are:

- To allow you and your child time to calm down during emotionally intense situations.

- To teach your children how to control their behavior when they get angry and upset.

The first part of Teaching Self-Control – Calming Down – is geared toward reducing the intensity of the interaction so that both of you can work on resolving the situation. The second part – Follow-Up Teaching – gives you an opportunity to teach your child some acceptable options for behaving when angry and upset.

Teaching Self-Control emphasizes giving clear descriptions of your child's behaviors, using consequences, teaching your child the correct behavior, and practicing it. Teaching Self-Control gives both you and your child a chance to calm down when tempers have flared. When everyone has some time to calm down before teaching continues, kids are more likely to learn how to share their feelings in appropriate and constructive ways. Here are the steps of Teaching Self-Control.

Part One: Calming Down

1. Describe the problem behavior.
2. Offer options to calm down.
3. Allow time to calm down.

Part Two: Follow-Up Teaching

1. Describe the positive behavior.
2. Practice.
3. Give a negative consequence.

It's never easy to remain calm when your child is very angry and being openly defiant and disrespectful. What's important is to first focus on helping the child calm down and regain self-control before you address the original problem behavior. Each of the steps of Teaching Self-Control is a way for parents to tell if the child is ready to cooperate and eventually get back to the initial problem that caused the blow-up in the first place. Not only do these steps act as markers of your child's ability to remain calm, they give parents a proven method to avoid being drawn into power struggles, escalating arguments, or an unsafe family situation.

Now, let's look at the steps to the first part of Teaching Self-Control, Calming Down, in more detail.

Describe the Problem Behavior

In a calm, level voice tone, briefly tell your child exactly what he is doing wrong. Your child probably will not be interested in listening to what you have to say at this time, so saying a lot won't help. Remember that you will have time to teach to the problem once your child settles down. Be clear and specific with what you do say. Don't speak too rapidly or say too much. For example, "John, you're yelling and glaring" gives the child a clear message about what he is doing.

Parents often say judgmental things when they dislike their child's behavior, such as, "Quit acting like a brat" or "I hate your lousy attitude." These critical, judgmental statements, however, only serve to fuel the emotional fire in your child. I suggest you simply describe what your child is doing wrong without yelling or being sarcastic or accusatory.

Using empathy also helps when your child is upset or angry. It shows that you understand your child's feelings. For example, you might say, "It looks like this is making you really upset." This starts the teaching sequence positively and shows your child that you really do care about his feelings. Plus, using empathy often helps your child see that you're focused on calming the situation down and not on placing blame or getting the upper hand.

Offer Options to Calm Down

The purpose of this step is to guide your child to make decisions that will help him to calm down. By giving your child simple, direct instructions you are setting limits for his behavior. Give simple instructions like "Please go to your room until you are calm" or "Go sit on the porch and cool down." Or, make calming statements to prompt your child: "Take a few deep breaths and try to settle down." Just as when you described the problem behavior, keep your words to a minimum. Don't give too many instructions or repeat them constantly; the child could perceive this as lecturing, badgering, or an opportunity to argue. Giving simple, clear options for calming down keeps the focus on having your child learn to self-calm.

It is very important that parents practice these first two steps. Practicing how to be brief, specific, calm, empathetic, and clear during intense situations is time worth investing. Besides giving your child an opportunity to regain self-control, clear messages and specific options on how to calm down help you avoid getting sidetracked into useless arguments or power struggles.

A child who learns two or three calming strategies and gets good at using them is more likely to respond to upsetting situations in an assertive manner. Here are some calming strategies and how to use and teach them:

Deep breathing

- Silently count to five as you take a deep breath in through your nose.
- Hold the breath for five seconds.
- Count to five again as you let the breath out slowly through your mouth.
- Take two normal breaths.
- Repeat the first four steps two or three times until you feel yourself calming down.
- Let me know when I check on you if you are calm.

Writing or drawing in a journal

- Go someplace where you won't be disturbed.
- Write down (or draw a picture that shows) how you are feeling and what you are thinking.
- Let me know when I check on you if you are calm.

Taking time to cool down

- Go to a place where you won't be disturbed or distracted.
- Take five minutes to calm down.
- If you need more time, calmly ask for it.
- Let me know when I check on you if you are calm.

Using positive self-talk

- Make a positive comment about how you can handle a situation appropriately. Use a phrase like, "I can get myself under control"; "I've done it before, I can do it again"; "If I stop now, things will get better"; or "I can do this."

- Repeat the statement you choose until you are calm.
- Let me know when I check on you if you are calm.

Muscle relaxation

- Clench and squeeze your fists for five seconds and slowly release them.
- Slowly roll your neck in circles for five seconds.
- Scrunch your shoulders and slowly roll them in circles several times.
- Slowly rotate your ankles.
- Raise your eyebrows as high as you can and slowly lower them.
- Scrunch your face and release.
- Let me know when I check on you if you are calm.

Allow Time to Calm Down

It's probably safe to say that giving children time to calm down may be a new concept to many parents. But if you remain calm and allow your children time to cool down, they are more likely to self-calm faster. Parents report that remembering this step has helped them to stay focused on getting the situation under control. Simply saying, "Let's take a little time to calm down. I'll be back in a few minutes," can be surprisingly effective. Sometimes giving you and your child a little "space" helps you both "save face."

As you take time to calm down, you can think of what you are going to teach next. This also allows the child to make a decision – to continue engaging in problem behavior or to calm down. Come back to the child as often as necessary. Ask questions like, "Are you ready to talk about what happened?" or "Have you calmed down enough to talk to me?"

Move to the next phase, Follow-Up Teaching, when your child is able to answer you in a reasonably calm voice and is willing to cooperate. You're not going to have the happiest child at this point, but it's important that he can pay attention and talk without losing self-control again.

If your child tries to use this "cool down time" as an opportunity to blare music, sleep, talk on the phone, or go from room to room disrupting others, then you should remind your child that this behavior will only make things worse for him later. For example, if your daughter gets angry when you tell her to turn off the TV and then refuses to stop watching, part of her consequence will be losing TV time. Don't make angry threats; simply inform your child that continued problem behavior will earn larger or more negative consequences. This is a good time to prompt your child to make better decisions and to give a brief reason that's meaningful to her.

It's important to take your time here. Give descriptions and instructions as needed to test your child's readiness to move on to Follow-Up Teaching. Most importantly, remain calm and in control of what you say and do. Following is a closer look at the steps to Follow-Up Teaching.

Describe the Positive Behavior

Start out by praising your child for calming down, then describe what your child can do differently next time to remain calm. Explain other, more positive ways to express frustration or anger. Children have to learn that if they get angry and blow up when something doesn't go their way, it leads to more negative consequences and less time doing the things they like. This is an opportunity to explain the prompts you gave in the "offer options to cool down" step and to encourage your child to remember how to calm down.

A good strategy for parents to use is the "Instead of..." phrase to describe positive behavior. It goes like this:

- *"*John, nice job calming down. Let's talk about what to do the next time you get mad. Instead of yelling and running out the door, the next time you get upset, please tell me you're mad and take a few deep breaths to calm down."

- "Sharon, you look and sound much calmer; nice work settling down. Let's talk about what to do next time you get upset. Instead of swearing, ask if you can sit on the porch until you are ready to talk about it."

The purpose of this phrase is to reinforce calming down and to teach children positive behavior they can use the next time they get upset. Part of this teaching can include helping them recognize when they are beginning to get upset and teaching them to say something like, "I'm getting mad. Can I have some time to calm down?"

Once children calm down, they can talk about the circumstances that triggered their anger and talk with you about a solution. If parents and kids can learn to talk about how they feel in these situations, they can successfully solve the problem rather than attack each other.

Practice

Once your child is able to talk with you calmly about what to do, it's important that she knows how to do it. Ask your child to take several deep breaths with you, count to ten, or repeat a request for time to calm down such as "I'm really upset right now. May I go to my room for a few minutes?" After the practice is over, let your child know what was done correctly and what needs improvement. Be as positive as you can be, especially if your child is making an honest effort to do what you ask. Practice allows you to see if your child is in control of her emotions and willing to cooperate with your instructions as well as to accept responsibility for the behavior.

Give a Negative Consequence

This is a crucial step to Teaching Self-Control. If there is a common mistake made by parents, it is that they forget to give a negative consequence for the out-of-control behavior. Some are so pleased to have the yelling stop that giving a consequence doesn't cross their minds. Other parents don't give a negative consequence because they don't want to anger or upset the child any further. Sometimes, after a blow-up is over, parents want to ease up or their children's remorse convinces the parents to forgo the consequence. These feelings are understandable, but they don't contribute to changing a child's behavior. Consequences do help change behavior, but only if you consistently use them.

With Teaching Self-Control, you should always give an appropriate negative consequence and follow through with it. Children must learn they cannot blow up or throw tantrums when things don't go their way. At school, these behaviors can result in detentions, suspensions, expulsions, or other disciplinary actions. At work, they could cost them their job. And most likely, children won't keep friends for very long if they can't control their tempers. As parents, we must teach children how to respond in less emotional and less harmful ways even when they get angry and upset. Consequences increase the effectiveness of your teaching, and the whole process of Teaching Self-Control helps your children learn better ways of managing their anger and how they behave when angry and upset.

Example of Teaching Self-Control

Let's take a look at an example of Teaching Self-Control:

Thirteen-year-old Tyler comes home from school upset over a low grade he received on a book report. When Tyler walks into the kitchen, his mom and his younger brother, James, are sitting at the table. James says, "Tyler, I got an 'A' on my spelling test today." Tyler slams his backpack on the table and replies, "Why don't you shut up. I don't care what you got on your stupid spelling test. You're just a f------ suck up."

Mom asks Tyler what's wrong. Tyler starts yelling about how his teacher is "stupid" and unfair because she gave him a "C" on his report. When Mom tries to start teaching to Tyler's problem behavior and what he said to his brother, Tyler continues to shout, then lunges toward James, and kicks him in the leg. Mom immediately steps between the boys, and tells Tyler he can either go to the living room or his bedroom. Tyler continues to yell as he leaves the room, so Mom tells him to stop shouting and try to calm down. She then goes over to check on James. When she sees he is okay, she asks him to go to the basement and watch TV so she can talk to Tyler, who is now shouting, swearing, and kicking the furniture in the living room. James leaves the kitchen, and Mom starts Teaching Self-Control with Tyler.

Part One: Calming down

1. Describe the problem behavior.

- Use empathy and understanding.
- Clearly and calmly describe the problem behaviors.

MOM: "Tyler, thanks for leaving the kitchen when I asked. I understand why you are mad, but yelling at and kicking your brother are not okay. What you are doing now is yelling, swearing, and kicking the furniture. You know that none of that is okay."

2. Offer options to calm down.

- Describe what you want him to do.
- Give options for calming down.

MOM: "Tyler, you can stay here or go to your room and calm down. I'll check on you in a few minutes to see if you're ready to talk about this. I suggest you take a few deep breaths and think about what you're doing."

TYLER: "This is so d--- stupid. Just leave me alone!"

Tyler goes to his room and slams the door shut.

3. Allow time to calm down.

- Give each of you a chance to calm down. (Take a few minutes to catch your breath. Come back to check on your child's safety and ask him if he is willing to talk.)
- Check for cooperative behavior.

After five minutes, Mom goes to Tyler's room and knocks on the door.

MOM: "Tyler, are you ready to talk with me about what happened when you came home?"

TYLER (IN A CALM VOICE): "You can come in."

(When the child is following your instructions and is willing to talk with you about the problem, move from the Calming Down phase to Follow-Up Teaching.)

Part Two: Follow-Up teaching

4. Describe the positive behavior.

- Think of a better way your child can react when he gets upset.
- Describe what he can do differently.

MOM: "Tyler, here is what you can do the next time you get upset. I'd like you to use the calming strategy you agreed on. Take a few deep breaths and ask me without yelling if you can go to your room to think. You can listen to music quietly if that will help you calm down. You are not allowed to use your phone."

5. Practice

- Practice increases the chance that your child will learn what to do next time.
- Let him know how he practiced.

MOM: "Let's practice what you can do the next time you're upset over something. Let's pretend that you just got home from school and you're upset because you've got a ton of homework and you won't be able to play basketball after school. Tell me what you would say."

TYLER: "Mom, I'm mad because I've got a lot of homework. Can I go to my room and calm down?"

MOM: "Tyler, that was great. You asked to go to your room, and you looked at me and used a nice voice. That's exactly what you should do whenever you're upset."

6. Give a negative consequence.

- Help prevent the problem from occurring again.

MOM: "We do have consequences for yelling at and kicking other people. So you've lost television for two nights. I'd also like you to go apologize to your brother. When you're done, bring your report back here and we'll go over it together."

In real-life situations, your child probably won't cooperate this quickly. He may go from arguing and swearing to being calm, and then suddenly start arguing again. Some kids have a lot of stamina when they're upset so it's best to realize it could take a while to resolve the problem. You may also have other distractions to deal with in these situations: Your other children need something, the phone rings, the pasta is boiling over on the stove, and so on. Interactions with your child do not occur in a void; other things are always taking place that affect your behavior. In those instances where other children are present, have them go to another area you have discussed with them ahead of time so the upset child doesn't have an audience, and adapt the teaching steps and your teaching style to the situation. Stick to simple descriptions and instructions, continue to use empathy, and stay calm. Also, when children misuse privileges when they're upset (blaring music on their CD players), they should lose access to those privileges (no CD or music player for the rest of the day) as part of the consequence.

Helpful Hints

Stay on task.

Don't lose sight of what you're trying to teach. Implement all of the steps of Teaching Self-Control. Concentrating on your child's behavior is much easier when you have a framework to follow. Teaching Self-Control gives you that framework. It helps you stay calm and avoid arguments that take you away from what you want to teach.

Your children may try to argue with what you say or call you names. They may say you don't love them or tell you how unfair you are. They may say things to make you feel guilty or angry or useless. Expect these statements but don't respond to them. If you get caught up in all of these side issues, you lose sight of your original purpose – to calm your child and to teach self-control. And, you can lose sight of the original problem and how you need to deal with it. If you find yourself responding to what your child is saying, remember to use a key phrase: "We'll talk about that when you calm down." Staying on task ensures that you won't start arguing or losing your temper.

Be aware of your physical actions.

These times can be emotionally explosive. Don't use threatening words or gestures that might encourage aggression or physical retaliation from your child. Some parents find that sitting down rather than standing helps to calm the situation. When they stand up – particularly fathers – children see them as more threatening. Any action your child views as aggressive will only make matters worse and reduce the likelihood that he or she will calm down.

Pointing your index finger, putting your hands on your hips, scowling, leaning over your child, and raising a fist are all examples of physical actions that tend to increase tension in these volatile situations. Try your best to avoid these gestures. Keep your hands in your pockets or fold your arms across your chest – just find something to do with hands and arms other than waving them at your child.

Plan consequences in advance.

Think of a variety of appropriate negative consequences beforehand, especially if losing self-control is a problem for your child. Making decisions when you are upset can lead to giving huge consequences that you can't follow through with.

Find time when your child is not upset to explain the consequence for arguing and fighting with you. You might say, for example, "Maria, when I tell you 'No,' sometimes you argue with me. Then you get real mad and start yelling. From now on, if you do this, you will lose your phone and computer privileges for two nights." Then explain to Maria why she needs to accept decisions and why she shouldn't argue or scream. Knowing what the consequence will be may help your child to think before losing self-control in the future.

Follow up with your child.

As your child calms down and you complete the teaching sequence, other side issues can arise. Some situations may call for an understanding approach. Kids may cry after an intense situation. They just don't know how to handle what they're feeling inside. When this happens, you might say, "Let's sit down and talk about why you've been feeling so angry. Maybe I can help. At least, I can listen."

Some children enjoy "making up" with parents after an emotionally intense situation. In these situations use a firm, emphatic ending to Teaching Self-Control and keep your follow-up brief. This discourages them from losing control in order to engage in hugs and kisses once everything calms down. Simply indicate that the child's behavior is unacceptable and that your interaction is finished: "Okay, we've practiced what to do. Now, go to your brother's room and apologize to him."

Whatever approach you take will be determined by your common sense and judgment. It depends entirely on how you feel about the situation and what you want to teach.

Earlier, we emphasized that you shouldn't get sidetracked with complaints and accusations that kids may bring up when they are angry. But that's only during the Teaching Self-Control process. Afterwards, when everyone has calmed down, you should discuss with your child those statements that upset or concerned you. This is your opportunity to find out the reasons behind the outburst.

Kids may make more negative comments during these emotionally intense situations especially when you first start using Teaching Self-Control because these words may have distracted you before. They may think they can avoid getting a consequence or doing what was asked if they just keep the pressure on you. In other situations, kids may make these comments because they sincerely don't know how to express their feelings in healthy ways. Sometimes, children later tell their parents that they made negative comments just because they were mad. Other times, kids really do have concerns, or they feel frustrated. Some children won't have a clue why they said what they did, but discussing it and allowing them to share their feelings helps them learn these kinds of statements are not acceptable and reassures parents about their child's true feelings.

When you have finished Teaching Self-Control and both you and your child are calm, you may want to discuss some of these comments. Tell your child that you're concerned about what was said. For younger children, remind them of what they said and ask if they meant it. For older children and teens, talk about trust. Ask your child or teen to share feelings and opinions with you. Regardless of why the comments were made, take time to hear what your child has to say. Whenever possible, implement the suggestions the child makes. By doing so, you will be opening the door to more constructive conversations with your child. You will also be reducing the likelihood that your child will express negative feelings in destructive ways.

Also, parents need to share with their older children and teens how they feel and their need to trust them. This open dialogue provides parents and children with a safe and more effective way to communicate what they really think without feeling hurt or rejected. Working through these rough times together helps form tight emotional bonds between you and your kids.

Finally, as part of following up, you should sit down with your child at a neutral time (when she is not angry or upset) and choose or develop a calming strategy for the child. This involves selecting a method of calming down. Having a strategy helps children recognize when they are beginning to feel angry or upset and familiarizes them with ways to stay calm. Then, when you must use Teaching Self-Control, your child may need only a prompt from you to realize that it's time to get negative emotions under control.

Parents must have a bountiful supply of patience if their children have problems with anger and loss of self-control. The wisest parents are those who realize that teaching their kids self-control is an ongoing process. It takes a long time. Don't try to rush the learning process; expecting too much too soon can create more problems than it solves. Be attentive to small accomplishments; praise even the smallest bit of progress your child makes. (And while you're at it, give yourself a big pat on the back! Teaching self-control is a tough job.) Look for small positive changes over time. Your child should have fewer angry outbursts, and the outbursts should be shorter and not nearly as intense. Teaching Self-Control helps parents and children break the painful cycle of arguments and power struggles. When tension is greatest in the family, Teaching Self-Control gives everyone a constructive way to resolve problems.

CHAPTER 19

WHEN IT'S MORE THAN JUST ANGER

Parents who have a child who regularly uses anger and aggression to get what he or she wants or to settle differences have a challenging journey ahead. They love their child and want to help change the angry behavior, but they don't know how. So the child's problem behaviors continue and perhaps worsen, the parents become frustrated by their inability to "fix" the problem, and family relationships are strained and damaged.

The purpose of this book is to help parents and children who face this kind of dilemma. One message I want to give parents is this: Don't give up on your kids. Don't give up hope for change. It can happen with the right plan and the right tools. The teaching methods and suggestions I've discussed in this book are the starting points for a new way to reach your children. They are practical, easy-to-use, and most importantly, effective. And they work because large numbers of parents have successfully used them to help their kids change their behaviors for the better.

I don't claim to have all the answers; when it comes to working with children who are angry, there are no guarantees or "miracle cures." Every family's problems are different, and preventing or reducing anger and aggression takes time and lots of effort. Parents and children have to learn to trust each other and work together. And changing your children's behavior likely means changing your own behavior. Those are huge tasks. How well you adapt what's in this book to your situation and your parenting style will contribute to how successful you will be.

In some cases, a child may need more help than parents can provide. When behavior becomes so serious or violent that the child poses a danger to self or others, immediate action is important. If you find yourself in this situation, your child's safety and the safety of others is critical. When imminent harm is the concern, take your child to an emergency room (ER) for an evaluation or call the police for assistance. Staff at the ER (or the police) can help determine if your child needs the immediate assistance provided by inpatient treatment.

If your child seems to be angry all the time and you are having little success changing that behavior using the strategies suggested in this book, counseling, therapy, or other interventions may be necessary. Parents must be willing to accept these situations and find appropriate help. This isn't an easy decision, but loving parents understand that tough decisions have to be made sometimes for the good of their children.

Sometimes, the anger children and teens express represent more than just being mad. Anger and irritability might be symptoms of more serious problems. For example:

- Kids who are struggling to adjust to significant life events often exhibit angry and irritable behavior.
- Some behavioral disorders, like Oppositional Defiant Disorder and Conduct Disorder, are characterized by anger and problem behaviors. Children and teens with these disorders are often argumentative, engage in rule-breaking behavior, exhibit aggression, along with other behavioral and emotional symptoms. These children often

need and benefit from more intensive treatment than parents can provide.

- Children who struggle with Attention Deficit/ Hyperactivity Disorder (ADHD) may also exhibit difficulties managing anger. ADHD may impair your child's ability to think before acting and to consider the consequences of actions before engaging in them. Working to reduce a child's impulsivity may help reduce problems related to anger as well.

- Anger for the anxious child may be a way to escape or avoid anxiety-producing situations. This might include anger and aggression in social situations, because interacting with other children is really difficult. If the child is angry or aggressive, other children will leave him or her alone. And for these youth, alone is easier or preferred over being with other children. Facing something you are extremely fearful of is difficult. For example, if someone told you that you have to confront your fear of snakes or spiders or heights or flying, how do you think you would respond? The typical response is resistance and irritability. And when pushed further, anger and aggression show up. Your children and teens are no different. So overcoming fears, worries, and anxieties that interfere with day-to-day life often requires additional support through outpatient treatment services.

- Children who feel like they have to do certain behaviors over and over or have things done in a specific way to reduce their anxious feelings may resort to anger or aggression to make sure they get to do the certain repetitive behavior(s). Or, they might exhibit anger as an expression of the intense internal distress they are experiencing because they were not able to do the specific ritual behavior(s) or action(s). Such behavior is common for children and teens with Obsessive Compulsive Disorder or Pervasive Developmental Delays like Autism. When these behaviors interfere with daily functioning, additional help is often needed.

• Anger may be a symptom or expression of a sad or depressed mood. When children and teens experience a depressed mood, they may not appear sad; instead, they may look like they are angry or irritable. Seeking outside assistance to help determine if your child or teen might be experiencing a depressed mood will help you and your child learn what is causing the anger and what to do about it.

These examples show there can be other, more serious, and complex issues at the root of your child's anger. If you have tried the strategies in this book or are concerned your child may be struggling with some of these issues, seeking professional services is a good idea. Outpatient behavioral health services may be sufficient to help your child. For some children and teens, outpatient services are not sufficient; they might require medication to help address their behavior and mood problems.

One way to think about the services available to parents and their children is on a continuum. At one end of the continuum are the least restrictive services available, while the opposite end of the spectrum includes the most restrictive ones. Restrictiveness refers to how much the service disrupts the child's typical day-to-day activities and life. The least restrictive services include things like parent training classes or outpatient behavioral health services. The most restrictive services include inpatient psychiatric hospitalization and intensive residential services. (To learn about the programs and services Boys Town offers, visit BoysTown.org.)

Children are our future. What they learn from you now will affect them for the rest of their lives. I have confidence in your abilities as a good parent. I know you love and care about your children, and that you want what's best for them. Give yourself a pat on the back for working hard to make their (and your family's) future brighter and happier.

INDEX

-A-

Acceptance, 67-70, 72-73, 75
Accepting "No" Answers, 123-124
Accountability, 169
Admiration, conveying, 71
Aggression, 23, 25-26, 29, 34, 95, 100, 116, 149, 177-179, 190, 213
  desensitizing, 151
  physical, 30-31, 37, 46-48, 117-118, 125-132, 168, 178, 193, 208
  verbal, 30-33, 36-37, 44, 46, 48, 99, 118, 168, 178, 193, 195, 201-203, 207
Anger, 13-15, 17-20, 25-27, 69-70, 149, 193, 213
  at different ages, 31-38
  controlling, 29
  definition of, 21
  expressing, 22-23, 30, 36, 41, 70, 89, 100, 102, 115-119, 129
  getting to the bottom of, 47-49
  help with, 49, 54, 63-64, 214-216
  justifying, 23-24
  managing, 86, 95
    assertively, 24-27, 39, 128, 130-131
    strategies for, 86-88
    teaching, 89, 177-190
  modeling, 38-40, 60, 85-88, 129
  parenting styles and, 60-61
  parents and, 30, 48, 63, 86-88
  reasons for, 41-49, 216
  response to, 38, 48
    appropriate, 38, 40
  school-age children and, 21-27, 33, 44-46, 182, 192

staying calm when, 38-39,
193-194
teenagers, 34-38, 47-48,
99-100, 184-185, 191, 203-
206
toddlers and, 31-32, 43
triggers for, 41-43, 44, 48,
196
identifying, 48-49
Anxiety, 14, 18, 24
Appreciation, 67, 71-73, 75
Approval, 67, 70-73, 75, 79
communicating, 70
Attention, 82-84
focused, 105
positive, 82, 105
Attention Deficit/Hyperactivity
Disorder (ADHD), 215
Autism, 215

-B-

Behavior
describing, 32, 79, 105-106,
109, 131, 145, 184-185,
196-198, 201-202, 205-206
goals, 125-132
learned, 122, 132, 148, 170
modeling, 18, 34, 85-97, 102,
193-194
monitoring, 37, 117
negative, 90-91, 119, 132,
142-143, 192, 195-196, 204
addressing, 32-34, 71, 103,
118, 122, 145-146, 190
reacting to, 76, 82-83, 90
teaching to, 177-190
positive, 75-76, 122
how to recognize, 77-80,
177

ignoring, 82
recognizing positive, 38,
63, 75-85, 107-109
reinforcing, 76-80, 82, 110
teaching new, 34
Blame game, 23-25
Boundaries, 115-119, 150
Boys Town, 216
Center for Behavioral Health,
140
Common Sense Parenting,
63-64

-C-

Calm(ing),
down, 36, 82, 101, 133-135,
181, 186, 189, 196-197,
200-201, 207
remaining, 18, 38, 86-88,
102, 108, 110, 112, 116,
142, 145, 194-197
strategies, 133-136, 135-139,
179, 181, 204
physical, 133-136, 199,
200, 204
thinking, 133-134, 136,
199-200
using charts for, 136-139
Child Protective Services, 117
Chores, 47, 103, 189
refusal to complete, 23, 47,
92-93
Communication, clear, 86,
99-113, 179-180, 182
with school-age children,
108-111
with teenagers, 111-113
with toddlers, 104-108
Conduct Disorder, 214

Confidence, 15, 18, 115
Consequences, 27, 83, 148,
    180, 182, 184-186, 189-190,
    192-193
    appropriate, 81, 91-97
    earning back, 188
    effective, 91-97
    immediate, 112, 118
    negative, 18, 23, 27, 60,
        96-97, 99-100, 107-108,
        110-111, 115, 128, 181,
        187, 202-203, 206
        delivering, 32, 61, 117
        earning, 34, 36
    planning, 208
    positive, 27, 181
    punishers, 89
    reinforcers, 89-90
    using, 89-97, 196
Consistency, 26-27, 54, 64, 66,
    128, 143, 188-190
Criticism, 23, 38, 66
    self-, 100-101
Curfew, 21-22, 90, 111, 128

-E-

Embarrassment, 15, 21, 23-24,
    33, 97
Emotions,
    assertiveness and, 24-27
    at different ages, 15-18,
        21-27
    expressing, 13-14, 20, 22-30,
        195, 210
    labeling, 13-15
    managing, 18-20, 27, 169
    modeling, 18-19, 24, 26-27
    "negative," 15, 17, 122
    "positive," 13-15, 17

primary, 21-23
recognizing, 33
responding to, 13-14
secondary, 21-24
Empathy, 19-20, 198, 207
Excitement, 13, 17, 19
Expectations, 15, 37
    communicating, 26-27, 35,
        115-119, 130, 148
    inconsistent, 59-60
    setting, 35, 59, 121-132
Extracurricular activities, 55-56,
    111

-F-

Fear, 13-15, 22-23, 33
Follow-Up Teaching, 196-198,
    200-201, 205-206, 209-211
Following Instructions, 77-78,
    108, 116, 123-124, 178-180,
    193
Friman, Dr. Pat, 67, 140
Frustration, 14, 19-21, 23-24,
    54, 69, 121, 213
    parent, 42-43, 48, 88, 106,
        111
    tolerance, 57

-G-

Grounding, 61, 90-91
Guilt, 14, 54

-H-

Happiness, 13, 15, 17-18
Homework, 34, 37, 47

-K-

Kindness, 172-173

-L-

Language, 33, 46
  foul, 33, 36-37, 126-128, 191
Limits, setting, 59, 119, 155-156
Listening, 69, 115, 149, 188
  active, 112
  to children, 99-113
Love, 22-23, 115, 142, 165, 169
  communicating, 65, 103, 113-114
  expressions of, 65-67
  unconditional, 64-67, 75

-M-

Media, 94, 147-155, 163
  controlling exposure to, 148, 153
  cyberbullying, 149
  Internet, 37, 147, 151-152, 154-155
  kids and, 149-155
  social, 148-149
  television watching, 150-152, 155
Monitoring children's location, 163-165, 179
Morals/values, 168-169, 171, 173

-N-

No Room for Bullies, 45

-O-

Obsessive Compulsive Disorder, 215
Oppositional Defiant Disorder, 214

-P-

Parent(ing)
  becoming a better, 53-73
  fundamentals of, 64
  goals, 54-56
  inconsistency in, 59-60
  styles, 55, 56-60
    anger and, 60-61
    authoritarian, 56-57, 60
    authoritative, 56, 58-59, 61-62
    changing, 62-63
    permissive, 56-58, 61-62
    taking stock of, 62
    three A's of, 67-72
    angry children and, 72-73
  training, 33
Parenting.org, 64
Pervasive Developmental Delays, 215
Pets, 169
Police intervention, 37, 138
Practice, 122-125, 130, 131-132, 145, 183, 185, 202, 206
Praise, 19, 38, 63, 77-81, 83-84, 105, 112, 118, 124-125, 144, 159, 189
  physical touch as, 79
  verbal, 78-80
Privileges, 40, 189, 207
  access to, 59, 94
  phone, 37, 42
Proactive Teaching, 118, 121-132
  aggressive kids, 125-132
  definition, 125
  examples of, 130
  teens and, 130

Problem-solving
POP, 159-161
examples of, 160-161
SODAS, 157-165
examples of, 161-162
strategies, 27
teaching, 157-165
Punishment, 60, 82, 97, 109

-R-

Rationales/reasons, 79-80, 112, 123, 131, 183, 185
other-centered, 187
self-centered, 186-187
Respect, 168-169
Responsibility, accepting, 69, 178, 179
Rewards, 78, 82
tangible, 79
vs. bribes, 80-82
Rules, 34, 115, 118, 141
enforcing, 42-43, 110-111
posting, 117
writing up, 116-117

-S-

Sadness, 13-15, 17-18, 21
School-age children,
anger and, 21-27, 32-34, 44-46, 90-91, 129, 182, 192
calming strategies for, 136-139
communicating with, 108-111
teaching to, 121-125
Self-calm, 14, 26, 198
learning how to, 39
Self-control, 106, 185, 208
losing, 191-211

regaining, 198
teaching, 193-194, 207, 209-210
example of, 203-204
when to use, 195-196
Self-harm, 17, 29, 100, 178, 214
Self-quiet, 14, 39-40, 139-140
Spirituality, 167-173
anger and, 169-171
modeling, 171-172
reasons for, 168-169

-T-

Tantrums, 31, 58, 62, 77, 81, 90, 95
appeasing, 13-14
ignoring, 92
preventing, 19
prior to, 31
reasons for, 31-32, 43
Teenagers, 121
anger and, 18-19, 34-38, 47-48, 90-92, 99-100, 102, 129, 184-185, 191, 203-206
brain development, 36
calming strategies for, 136-139
clothes, 57, 59, 94
communicating with, 111-113
friends, 34-35, 37, 57
identifying potential, 57
independence, 35-37, 59
teaching to, 121-125
Time-out, 32, 91-92, 107-108, 118, 128, 180, 182
duration of, 141
guidelines, 140-145
location for, 140-141

post-, 142-143
toddlers and, 139-144
when to use, 142-144
Toddlers
anger and, 31-32, 43
communicating with, 104-108
language, 32
time-out and, 139-144
Trust, 35-36, 112

-V-

Voice tone, 38, 107, 129, 180,
200-201

-W-

Worry, 14-15, 21-23